MW01689496

Growing in CHRIST®

Lower Elementary Teacher Guide

CONCORDIA PUBLISHING HOUSE • SAINT LOUIS

God Protects His People in Egypt and the Exodus

OLD TESTAMENT 2

3558 S. Jefferson Ave., St. Louis, MO 63118-3968

1-800-325-3040 • www.cph.org

Written by Angela Embretson (Lessons 6–11), Carol Hinz (Lessons 1–5), Brenda Trunkhill (Lessons 12–13); Gail E. Pawlitz, consultant

Edited by Gail E. Pawlitz and Brenda Trunkhill

Manufactured in the United States of America

Growing in Christ® is published by Concordia Publishing House. Your comments and suggestions concerning this material are appreciated. Email us at sundayschool@cph.org.

Contents

Introduction

For the New User

The Lower Elementary level of Growing in Christ is an early-reader version for ages 6 through 8. It includes a Teacher Guide, Teacher Tools (a packet of materials for teachers), and Student Pack (a packet of materials for children).

Features of the Teacher Guide

- An easy-to-use, four-step lesson plan
- Weekly activity pages to supplement the lessons and engage students in additional projects or activities
- A weekly Bible study for the teacher titled "Preparing the Lesson"
- Age-appropriate ways to teach the Bible story and apply it to young lives
- Perforated pages to make team teaching or small- and large-group teaching easier

Teacher Tools

This packet provides resources vital to effective teaching:

- **Posters** (teaching aids and pictures)
- **Storytelling Figures** (four pages of figures for use in telling the Bible stories)
- **Table Tent Backgrounds** (two background scenes for use with storytelling figures)
- **Attendance Chart**
- **CD** with recordings of hymns, songs, Bible Words, catechism songs, and Bible stories; melody-line scores for all music on the CD; Activity Pages, Resource Pages, and a list of the student Bible Words and song lyrics

Student Pack

You will need one for each child. This packet includes the following materials:

- **Student Book,** which contains the Bible Words, the Lesson Leaflets, and the Craft Pages
- **Sticker Pages**—three perforated pages with sections that can be separated
- **CD** with recordings of songs, hymns, catechism songs, and Bible Words songs

Additional Materials

In addition to the items on the "Materials Needed" list in the Teacher Guide, you will also need your Bible, catechism, hymnal, children's songbook *Songs of God's Love* (*SGL*) , an offering basket, and CD player each week, as well as other standard classroom supplies, such as scissors, tape, glue, paper, and crayons or markers. You may wish to use a device for recording and displaying media. You may also wish to order the following helps from Concordia Publishing House (call 1-800-325-3040 for cost information and to order):

- **Puppet**: Lily (a little girl; order no. 41-1028)
- **Puppet (*optional*)**: Sprout (a little boy; if you do not have a Sprout puppet, Jelly makes a good substitute; order no. 57-1115)

- ***My First Hymnal:*** This is a great source of hymns for this age level (order item number 99-2268).
- ***Sing & Wonder: Songs and Activities Based on the Apostles' Creed:*** (order item number 22-3170)
- ***Wiggle & Wonder: Bible Story Rhymes and Finger Plays:*** (order item number 22-3130)
- **Restickable glue stick*:*** to allow for repeat use in attaching story figures to backgrounds (order online at cph.org, or find in the office supply section of your local discount store)
- **Church Year Worship Kit*:*** This is a great resource for teaching children about the Church Year (includes a Leader Guide, an altar poster with paraments and more, prayer posters, and a CD)
- ***Arch Books***—CPH has the following books that relate to Bible accounts this quarter; consider using them for Bible story presentation or review, or have them available before class.

Lesson 1	*Joseph: Jacob's Favorite Son*	59-2233
Lesson 2	*Joseph: Jacob's Favorite Son*	59-2233
Lesson 3	*Joseph: Jacob's Favorite Son*	59-2233
Lesson 4	*Joseph: Jacob's Favorite Son*	59-2233
Lesson 5	*Tiny Baby Moses*	59-1550
Lesson 7	*The Ten Plagues*	59-1608
Lesson 9	*Moses' Dry Feet*	59-1518
Lesson 10	*Moses and the Long Walk*	59-1607
Lesson 11	*The Ten Commandments*	59-1586
Lesson 13	*Moses and the Bronze Snake*	59-2219

Teaching Helps

You can find many teaching helps, including updates, training helps, and links to podcasts and other resources for your weekly preparation and teaching at our Sunday School website, **cph.org/sundayschool.**

Lesson 1

Date of Use

Preparing the Lesson

Joseph and His Brothers

Genesis 37

Key Point

Joseph was hated by his brothers, who threatened him with death and sold him into slavery, but he was rescued by God. God's Son, Jesus, was also hated and was killed for our sin. He is our deliverer from sin, death, and the power of the devil.

Law/**Gospel**

Hatred ruins relationships and separates me from others and from God. **Jesus' death and resurrection restores my relationships with God and others.**

Context

Rachel died as her second son, Benjamin, was born. The twelve tribes of Israel are complete, but Jacob's favored wife is dead. Now Jacob's favor rests with Joseph, Rachel's firstborn. Jacob saw his father, Isaac, before he died and now lives in his father's land, the land of Canaan. The sons of Israel are shepherds.

Commentary

The account of Jacob begins and ends with Joseph (Genesis 37:2; 46:4). God always provides a deliverer for His people. In the lifetime of Jacob, Joseph was the deliverer. Moses records the Christlike characteristics of Joseph in Genesis, his first book. Joseph is never depicted as sinning in his vocation. He was not sinless, of course, for there would be only one Sinless One, Jesus Christ. Instead we see Joseph fulfilling his God-given vocations faithfully, trusting in God's mercy.

As a son, Joseph reports the misdeeds of his father's other sons. As a servant to Potiphar, Joseph becomes chief of all his master's possessions and remains chaste despite the advances of Potiphar's wife. In prison, he manages the jail with diligence, becoming a leader among inmates. As the right hand of Pharaoh, Joseph rules with wisdom and mercy. Finally, as a brother, Joseph forgives all that his brothers meant for evil because he saw the hand of God working for good. In each vocation—son, worker, and brother—Joseph trusted God to provide him with all that he needed to support his body and life, to defend him against all danger, and to guard and protect him from all evil (Small Catechism, First Article).

Joseph bore the cross of being his father's well-beloved son. He incurred the wrath of his other brothers. God revealed to Joseph the future, yet his brothers, his father, and his mother refused to believe him. They even rebuked him. But just as Mary pondered strange and wonderful things in her heart (Luke 2:19, 51), so Jacob kept the matter of these dreams in mind (Genesis 37:11).

Joseph's cross was magnified by his brothers' betrayal into death. They cast him into a pit, while dreaming up a story of vindication. When greed overcame their desire for blood, they sold him into slavery. Reuben's weakhearted attempts were too little and too late. He valued favor with his brothers more than the life of his father's son. Good intentions do not produce good works. What humans mean for evil, God uses for good.

To hear an in-depth discussion of this Bible account, visit cph.org/podcast and listen to our Seeds of Faith podcast each week.

Lesson 1

Joseph and His Brothers

Genesis 37

Connections

Bible Words
For those who love God all things work together for good. Romans 8:28

Faith Word
deliverer

Hymn
Praise God, from Whom All Blessings Flow (*LSB* 805; CD 3)

Catechism
Fifth and Tenth Commandments
Lord's Prayer: Seventh Petition

Liturgy
Post-Communion Canticle Thank the Lord and Sing His Praise (*SGL*, p. 41; CD 16)

1 Opening (10 minutes)

Introducing Concepts

To Prepare: Post the attendance chart, and set out the offering basket and stickers (Student Pack).

Greet your students as they arrive. Introduce yourself to any new students, and have the other children introduce themselves. While the children are talking, listen for special prayer requests. Use the stickers (Student Pack) to record attendance.

Prepare the children for today's lesson by introducing the concept that jealousy and hatred between people ruin relationships. On the board or on a large piece of paper, draw two stick people with space in between them.

Say **In our Bible story today, some brothers are jealous of another brother because of his fancy clothes and irritating dreams. Let's imagine that these two stick figures are two brothers or two sisters or maybe two friends.** Draw a line (erasable) connecting the two figures. **Let's draw a line between them to show that they are friends. Isn't it wonderful to have a friend? However, sometimes, friends or brothers or sisters don't get along. Sometimes, one of them is jealous of the other. One person is unhappy or angry because they want what the other person has. They know the other person has something more or better than they have. Tell me what kind of things might make this person jealous of this other person.**

Invite the children to offer suggestions. As they share, little by little, erase part of the line between the two stick figures so that the line is broken (dashed).

MATERIALS NEEDED

1 Opening	2 God Speaks	3 We Live	4 Closing
Teacher Tools Attendance chart CD **Student Pack** Stickers **Other Supplies** Offering basket Resource Page 1 (TG) Songbook	**Teacher Tools** Poster E Background A Storytelling Figures Glue stick **Student Pack** Lesson Leaflet 1 **Other Supplies** Resource Page 2 (TG) Activity Page 1 (optional)	**Student Pack** Craft Page 1 White construction paper (optional) **Other Supplies** Songbook	**Teacher Tools** CD **Other Supplies** Songbook

Say **When two people don't get along because one of them is jealous of the other, their friendship is broken. Being jealous of someone can lead to feelings of hatred toward that person. When you hate someone, you might hurt him or her with your thoughts, words, or actions.**

Use the catechism to review the Fifth Commandment, reminding us not to physically hurt others and the Tenth Commandment, reminding us not to covet (desire) what others have.

In today's Bible story, bad things happen among brothers. After the Opening, we'll find out more about the brothers and how God was at work.

Save the drawing of the stick people to use again after the Bible story.

Rituals and Routines

To Prepare: If your class gathers with others for the Opening, begin the lesson with part 2. If you prefer to develop your own opening, a suggested outline follows. For an extended opening, use Resource Page 1 (TG).

Gathering Song: "God Is So Good" (*SGL*, p. 62; CD 8)

Invocation: **In the name of the Father and of the Son and of the Holy Spirit. Amen.**

Offering

The Commandments: Review the First Commandment (CD 19)

Prayers

Celebrations: Birthdays and Baptism birthdays

2 God Speaks (20 minutes)

Key Point

Joseph was hated by his brothers, who threatened him with death and sold him into slavery, but he was rescued by God. God's Son, Jesus, was also hated and was killed for our sin. He is our deliverer from sin, death, and the power of the devil.

Introducing God's Word

To Prepare: Set out a restickable glue stick (available from cph.org), the Faith Words Poster (Poster E), and the Faith Words cards (Resource Page 2) found in the back of the Teacher Guide. This week, cut out the word *deliverer* from the cards.

Begin with the following question.

Say **What kind of worker makes deliveries?** Give the children time to respond about people who bring things to you. **Sometimes, people deliver food such as pizza or ice cream. Sometimes, they deliver a service, such as fixing an air conditioner or rescuing people from a burning house. It is not always easy to deliver things. Some people have to learn skills and information before they can help others.**

In today's story, God chooses a young man to be a deliverer. Before he is old enough to be that deliverer, he goes through many troubles. God is with him during his troubles, and the troubles help him later in life. Through the troubles, he gets the skills he needs to do his work. Through the troubles, God puts him in the right country to help many people. Let's post the Faith Word *deliverer* and then listen to the Bible story about God's work in Joseph's life. Ask one of the children to use the glue stick to add the word *deliverer* to the Faith Words Poster.

Telling God's Word

To Prepare: Have the Background A of the Table Tent and storytelling figures for Lesson 1 ready. Use the glue stick to post the figures. Place a Bible near you.

Say **Today's Bible story, "Joseph and His Brothers," is from God's Word in the Book of Genesis.** Show the children where to find Genesis in the Bible. Place Joseph (1-1) on the background. **This is Joseph. He was Jacob's son. When he was seventeen years old, his job was to take care of the family's sheep with his ten older brothers.** Add ten brothers (1-2).

Joseph and his older brothers didn't get along. It could be because Joseph told his father bad things about his brothers, and this made the brothers angry. It could be because Jacob loved Joseph more than he loved any of his other sons. Jacob gave Joseph a coat with many colors. Put the coat (1-3) on Joseph. **After Joseph got his special coat, his brothers were jealous and could not even talk to him without getting angry.**

Something else made the brothers hate Joseph. It was his dreams. Joseph told his brothers, "We were tying up bundles of grain in the field. My bundle stood up straight. And your bundles all gathered around mine and bowed down to it." Add 1-4 anywhere near Joseph.

His brothers said, "Do you think you are going to rule over us?"

Then Joseph had another dream. He said to his brothers, "I dreamed the sun, the moon, and eleven stars were bowing down to me." Now the brothers hated Joseph because he seemed to be bragging that they would all bow down to him.

One day, Jacob sent Joseph to check on his brothers, who were taking care of sheep far from home. Before Joseph came near, his brothers saw him. In their anger, they planned to kill him. They said, "Here comes the dreamer. Let's kill him and throw him into one of the pits. Remove all figures. **Then we'll say that a wild animal has eaten him. We'll see if his dreams come true!" When Joseph arrived, they took off his robe and threw him into a pit.**

Later, the brothers saw a caravan of Ishmaelites (ISH may el ites) **coming with their camels. The Ishmaelites were traders who bought and sold things. They were on their way to Egypt.**

Instead of killing Joseph, the brothers decided to sell Joseph to the Ishmaelite traders. Add 1-5. **The brothers pulled Joseph out of the pit and sold him for twenty pieces of silver. The Ishmaelites took Joseph with them to Egypt.**

To hide their sin, the brothers found a way to lie to their father about Joseph. They dipped his coat of many colors in some blood from a goat and brought the robe home to their father, Jacob. Their father knew it was Joseph's coat. He thought a wild animal had killed Joseph.

The angry and jealous brothers kept their secret, and Jacob was sad for a long time. He did not know that Joseph was really alive or that, years later, God would use Joseph in Egypt to save many people.

Even though Joseph had many troubles, God was with him the whole time, preparing him for a big job. Later, God would use Joseph to save many people from starving. Joseph's dreams came true. He became a ruler and a deliverer. God used Joseph's difficult experiences for the good of Joseph, the people in the story, and even for us today.

Lesson Leaflet Review

Building Relationships!

To Prepare: From the Student Book, use Lesson Leaflet 1. As an optional review, make copies of Activity Page 1.

Discuss the leaflet painting. To do the review, open the leaflet. Children work with a partner to find the objects hidden in the big picture and then use them to retell the Bible story to each other.

When the children have finished,

Ask **Which object is not in the Bible story?** (The cross) **Even though you didn't hear about the cross in Joseph's story, God was at work in Joseph's life, preparing a way for Jesus to be born many years later. On the cross, Jesus died for our sins. There, He delivered us from sin, death, and the power of the devil and restored our relationship with God.**

As an optional review, use Activity Page 1.

Bible Words

For those who love God all things work together for good. Romans 8:28

To Prepare: Use a piece of craft paper. On one side in big letters, write the word *good*. Divide the other side of the paper into three parts. On one part, draw a simple coat. On the middle part, draw a stalk of grain. On the third part, draw a bag of money. Then, cut apart the three sections.

Distribute the three puzzle pieces to three students.

Front *Back*

Ask **What do you see on your paper?** After each child answers, continue. **Each picture on one side of your paper tells something about our Bible story, something about Joseph's early life. Some of those things were special—like getting a new coat. Others were not special at all—like being sold as a slave. What you don't see as easily is God at work. Let's put the three pieces together. We will find a word that tells what God was doing through the coat, the dreams, and the sale of Joseph.** Invite the three students to put their pieces together and form the word *Good*.

Say **Our Bible Words say that no matter what happens to God's children, He is always working it out for good. When you have troubles, God works it out to be good for you! You may never see how that happens, but you have God's promise that it will. God knows everything, and He knows what is best for us.**

Read the Bible Words together on the leaflet. Use the cues to help the children learn the Bible Words.

3 We Live (20 minutes)

Growing through God's Word

To Prepare: Use the drawing from Introducing Concepts (in the Opening). Set out full pieces of construction paper for making posters or wide strips of paper for making bookmarks (optional).

Point to the drawings on the board, or on the paper, used earlier.

Say **The broken lines remind us that sin separates us from one another.** You may want to search the Web for information about "jealousy" and "conflict resolution for young children"; discuss as a class. Write the word *God* above the stick figures. From the word *God*, draw a broken line to each stick figure. **Sin breaks our connection to God. By ourselves, we cannot fix the brokenness of sin.**

God loved us so much that He sent a Savior to deliver us from evil and fix all the brokenness sin causes. God sent His Son, Jesus, to the earth to make everything right between God and us again.

People were angry at Jesus and hated Him. Jesus suffered and died on the cross for our sins. But He rose again on Easter morning. His resurrection is proof that He has defeated our enemies. Who are those enemies? (Sin, death, and the devil) **What can we add to this drawing to help us remember that Jesus has done all this for us?** Let the children share their ideas.

Connect the broken lines. **Jesus is our deliverer. Through faith in Him, our sins are forgiven. We still have troubles and sadness. You will sometimes be angry at others and they will be angry at you, but Jesus fixes our relationships. We have Jesus and His victory on the cross. Because we have Jesus, God works all things for good in our lives. In our sadness, we don't always see that good. But we can rejoice and sing because we have God's promise. Through Jesus, our broken lives are healed.**

To remind the children of God's promise, give them time to decorate a poster or bookmark made with construction paper. Write the phrase "God uses all things for good in my life" on the board for students to copy onto their paper, or photocopy a piece of paper that has the phrase prewritten on it. Encourage the children to keep the bookmark in their Bible or to hang the poster on their wall to remind them of God's promise whenever they're facing troubles, sadness, or broken relationships.

16

Sing "Thank the Lord and Sing His Praise" (*SGL*, p. 41; CD 16)

Craft Page

Engaging Activity!

To Prepare: You will need Craft Page 1 and scissors.

Cut apart the cards. Use them to play a match game. Help the children find a partner to play with. Decide if you want to use one person's deck to keep the game shorter and simplified or combine the two decks to make it more challenging.

Turn the cards facedown, placing them in rows or columns. To begin, one player turns over two cards. If the pictures on the cards match, that player keeps the cards and recites the Bible Words. Then he or she tries to make another match. If the cards do not match, the other player takes a turn. Play continues until all the cards have been turned over.

4 Closing (5 minutes)

To Prepare: Use the CD. Gather materials to send home.

Gather the children for the Closing. Follow the same routine each week.

Say **God uses all things for good in your life.**

Sing "Praise God, from Whom All Blessings Flow" (*LSB* 805; CD 3)

Say **For those who love God all things work together for good** (Romans 8:28).

Challenge Challenge the children to work at mending any broken relationships they have. If they are mad at someone, challenge them to forgive the other person and, through Jesus, make things right again.

Pray **Dear God, thank You for sending Jesus to be my deliverer from sin and evil. Be with me in my troubles, and work things together for my good. In Jesus' name I pray. Amen.**

As the children leave, remind them:

Say **Jesus is your deliverer.**

Reflect Do you feel hurried during the time the students are leaving? Organize papers to send home as the lesson progresses.

Joseph and His Brothers

Choose a color for each answer

☐ True ☐ Not true

With a friend, read the sentences in each stripe. Decide if the sentences are true or not true.
Use the colors you have chosen to show your answers.

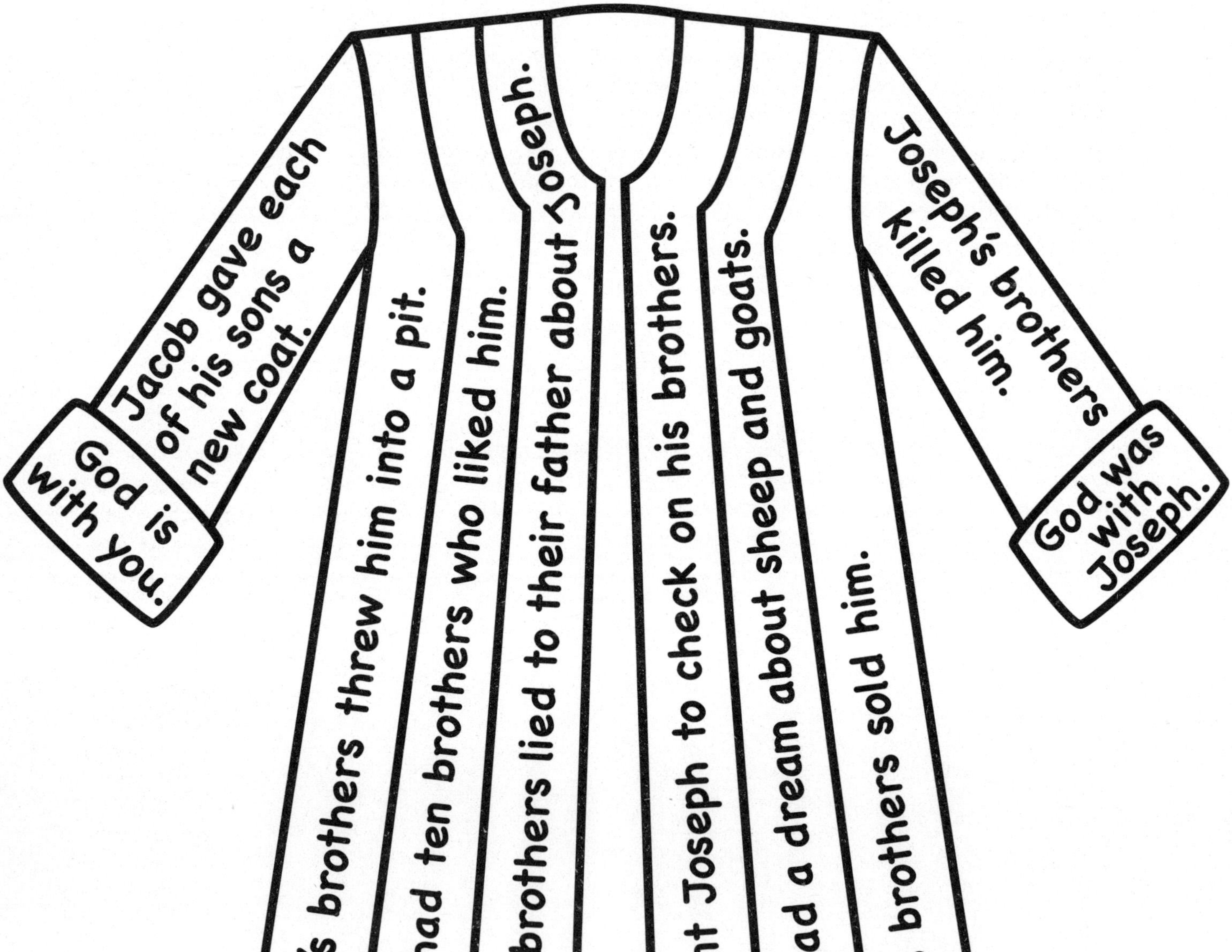

 Activity Page 1 Teacher: This page is also available on the CD in your Teacher Tools. Growing in Christ® Lower Elementary

Lesson 2

Preparing the Lesson

____
Date of Use

Joseph's Troubles

Genesis 39

Key Point

The Lord was with Joseph and, through him, saved Joseph's family and others. God promises to be with us in every situation, and through His Son, Jesus, a descendant of Joseph's brother Judah, God saves us from our sin.

Law/**Gospel**

I sin when I do not want to live out my vocation or forget that God is with me in my troubles; these sins, like all sin, condemn me to eternal death. **Nevertheless, God is with me in all my troubles and offers me and all who sin His steadfast love and mercy for the sake of His Son, Jesus.**

Context

Joseph's brothers get rid of the dreamer. The brothers cover up their evil with lies and blood, and Joseph's father refuses to be comforted. The sons of the Egyptian slave woman (Genesis 21:8–21; 39:1; Galatians 4:21–25) sell the favored son of their father into slavery. Against his will, Joseph becomes the leader of an Egyptian household. The Lord is with him.

Commentary

The theme of God's presence in all of Joseph's circumstances is central (Genesis 39:2, 3, 21, 23). The Lord is always working for the good of His own. Joseph serves Potiphar well. Joseph knows how to manage details and oversee things. "The Lord blessed the Egyptian's house for Joseph's sake" (Genesis 39:5)—every unbelieving one of them. God allows Joseph to suffer while allowing his evil brothers to get off free. He allows Potiphar and his indecent wife to prosper. All this God does for the purpose of preserving His people and working good for those who love Him.

Joseph knows and accepts his vocation. Potiphar's wife does not know her vocation. It is not Joseph's role to share intimacies with this woman. That is Potiphar's vocation. So Joseph says no to her ambush and invitations with a muscular "How then can I do this great wickedness and sin against God?" (Genesis 39:9). It is sin against God, against Potiphar, against her, and against Joseph's own body and calling. And so it is "wicked." That's the right word—God's word. Joseph rightly sees everything that this sin will touch, and he answers well. He still gets no reward for it.

In fact, Joseph receives another cross. His newest humiliation is to go down even further, into prison. The godly one suffers. The Lord is with him? Yes. God is doing something with Joseph in another vocation—this one in prison, with shackled feet and an iron collar around his neck (Psalm 105:17–22). All this looks forward to another vocation.

"The Lord was with Joseph," Genesis keeps repeating. He was with the slave Joseph, the seduced Joseph, and the shackled Joseph. Through it all, the Lord showed him steadfast love. Love—so the Lord could save His people at that time and bless the nations of the world through Jacob's other offspring. Love—so the Lord could show you Jesus, steadfast love incarnate. God did all that, with Joseph, for you.

To hear an in-depth discussion of this Bible account, visit cph.org/podcast and listen to our Seeds of Faith podcast each week.

Lesson 2

Joseph's Troubles

Genesis 39

Connections

Bible Words
God, the Lord, is my strength.
Habakkuk 3:19 (CD 7)

Faith Word
steadfast

Hymn
Praise God, from Whom All Blessings Flow
(*LSB* 805; CD 3)

Catechism
Lord's Prayer: Seventh Petition

1 Opening (10 minutes)

Introducing Concepts

To Prepare: Post the attendance chart, and set out the offering basket and stickers (Student Pack).

Greet your students as they arrive. Introduce yourself to any new students, and have the other children introduce themselves. While the children are talking, listen for special prayer requests. Use the stickers (Student Pack) to record attendance.

In this week's lesson, Joseph works hard and earns a good position in his master Potiphar's (PAHT uh fur) house. Potiphar's wife tempts him to sin, but Joseph says no. Potiphar's wife lies to her husband about Joseph. Potiphar has Joseph put in prison. The concept to develop is that we live in a sinful world, where the sins of others may cause us trouble; sometimes, we forget that God is with us in our troubles. Yet our Lord and Savior is with us as He was with Joseph.

When the children arrive, assign them to work with another child. The children are to make up a story where a child gets in trouble for doing something right. Give the children a few minutes to work together. Then ask them to share their idea or to act it out. When they have finished,

Say **In this week's Bible story, someone does something right and gets in trouble. As you listen, you will find out what happened and how God was at work.**

MATERIALS NEEDED

1 Opening	2 God Speaks	3 We Live	4 Closing
Teacher Tools Attendance chart CD **Student Pack** Stickers **Other Supplies** Offering basket Resource Page 1 (TG) Songbook	**Teacher Tools** Poster E Glue stick CD Poster A **Student Pack** Lesson Leaflet 2 **Other Supplies** Resource Page 2 (TG) Activity Page 2 (TG) Pictures of four objects Sticky note	**Student Pack** Craft Page 2 Stickers **Other Supplies** Lily the puppet Paper with Bible Words Songbook Key ring (optional) Cardstock (optional)	**Teacher Tools** CD **Other Supplies** Songbook

Use the catechism to review the Seventh Petition, where we ask God to deliver us from evil.

Rituals and Routines

To Prepare: If your class gathers with others for the Opening, begin with part 2 of this lesson. For an extended opening, use Resource Page 1 in the back of this book.

Gathering Song: "God, Our Father, Hear Your Children" (*SGL*, p. 67)
Invocation: **In the name of the Father and of the Son and of the Holy Spirit. Amen.**
Offering
The Commandments: Review the First Commandment (CD 19)
Prayers
Celebrations: Birthdays and Baptism birthdays

2 God Speaks (20 minutes)

Introducing God's Word

To Prepare: Set out a restickable glue stick (available from cph.org), the Faith Words Poster (Poster E), and the Faith Words cards (Resource Page 2) found in the back of the Teacher Guide. This week, cut out the word *steadfast* from the cards.

Ask all the children to stand up and move to one side of the room. Explain that in this activity, they may have to move from one side of the room to the other.

Active Learning Idea!

Say **If you have had a friend who was mean to you, move from this side of the room to the other side of the room.** Point in the direction that you want the children to move. **If you have ever felt that someone in your class liked you and then changed his or her mind and *didn't* like you, move to the other side of the room. God gave us families to love each other no matter what, but if you have ever *felt* that someone in your family didn't love you, move to the other side of the room.**

It is sad to feel excluded, overlooked, and unloved. God's love includes you at all times. He does not overlook you. God's love never changes. God's love for you is loyal and dependable. God's love for you is faithful and trustworthy. No matter what happens, God's love for you is constant. God calls His love steadfast. Today, we will hear about how God loved Joseph steadfastly.

Ask one of the children to add the word *steadfast* to the Faith Words Poster.

Telling God's Word

To Prepare: Show Poster A when you come to a special place in the Bible story reading. Have copies of Activity Page 2 and crayons available.

While the children are listening to today's Bible story, ask them to color Activity Page 2 when you describe which section to work on. Allow the children to work with a friend, if needed.

Say **Joseph was one of Jacob's sons. His brothers were jealous of him because Jacob loved Joseph the best.**

God gave Joseph dreams. In his dreams, Joseph saw that one day he would be a ruler. He didn't know when it was going to happen, but he knew that God had plans for him. On your page, color in the hearts that show smiling faces, because Joseph knew that God had plans for him.

One day, the brothers sold Joseph to some traders. The traders took Joseph to Egypt as their slave. A rich man named Potiphar bought Joseph. Poor Joseph. He could not go home, so he made the best of his situation. Now color in the sad faces. Joseph worked hard for Potiphar. His master saw that everything Joseph did, God blessed. Since Joseph was doing such a wonderful job, Potiphar put Joseph in charge of all his workers and all his things. Joseph was free to go anywhere, even inside the beautiful home of his master and the rooms of Potiphar's wife. Color in the hearts that show a Bible times home.

Potiphar's wife was a tricky woman who didn't love God. She wanted Joseph to do bad things. One day, she said, "Come with me. Let's do bad things together."

But Joseph wouldn't do it. He told Potiphar's wife, "I will not do it. My master trusts me to take care of his house and everything he has. How can I do this great wickedness and sin against God?"

Day after day, she kept talking to Joseph, trying to get him to do bad things. Day after day, Joseph would not listen to her. One day, when Potiphar was away, she grabbed Joseph by his coat and pulled him near her. She said, "You must do as I say."

Joseph wouldn't do it. He pulled himself free and ran away, but his coat was in her hands. Now Potiphar's wife did more wicked things. She began to scream and cry. Other servants came running. She lied and said that Joseph had hurt her.

When Potiphar came home, she told him the same story. She said, "Joseph hurt me." Show Poster A.

As soon as Potiphar heard his wife's story, he was angry. Potiphar put Joseph in the king's prison. Color in the hearts that show a prison window.

Even though Joseph had many troubles, the Lord was with Joseph and showed him steadfast love. The keeper of the prison liked Joseph and put him in charge of all the prisoners. The Lord was taking care of Joseph.

Joseph had many changes in his life. Through the sad times and happy times, through the hard times of temptation and joyous times of success, Joseph could be sure of one thing.

With a friend, read the letters written on the hearts. Find out what gift Joseph had throughout his entire life. The letters left on Activity Page 2 spell "God's steadfast love."

Lesson Leaflet Review

To Prepare: Hand out Lesson Leaflet 2 and a pencil, crayons, or markers to each child.

Discuss the illustration on the leaflet cover by answering the questions provided. Then, open the leaflet to the interior page. Help the students draw a line from the picture through (across) the heart to the sentence that tells what happened in the story.

Bible Words

God, the Lord, is my strength. Habakkuk 3:19

To Prepare: Bring to class pictures of four objects with increasingly heavier weights. One of the objects should be too heavy for any child to lift, but possible for an adult to lift. Instead of showing pictures, you can speak about four different things or even bring four different things and let four children try to lift them. Write the word *troubles* on a sticky note and attach it to the heaviest object.

One at a time with the students, examine each object (or picture) that you brought to class.

Ask **Can you lift this?** Wait for a response. **How could you do that?** (I could use my muscles. I am strong. It was light.)

When you get to the heaviest object, the children will not be able to lift it. After you read the word *troubles* on the note, tell how you could help.

Say **Look, this object has a note on it.** Read what the note says (troubles). **I could lift this object for you. I could use my strength.** Lift the object.

Our Bible Words for today tell us that God is our strength. With our own strength, we can't resist temptation and go on when we have troubles. God gave Joseph strength to endure troubles. Through it all—no matter what happened to Joseph—God was with Him and loved Him. God gives us His strength to resist temptations and endure our troubles.

Repeat the Bible Words, using the cues as a guide. Then, sing the Bible Words (CD 7).

Great Idea!

Key Point

The Lord was with Joseph and, through him, saved Joseph's family and others. God promises to be with us in every situation, and through His Son, Jesus, a descendant of Joseph's brother Judah, God saves us from our sin.

3 We Live (20 minutes)

Growing through God's Word

To Prepare: Use Lily to teach about how we are often tempted and troubled. Write the Bible Words on a piece of paper that will fit in Lily's satchel.

Teacher: Lily, I'm surprised to see you. Have you been here long?

Lily: Long enough to hear about Joseph's troubles. Poor Joseph. He had a bad, bad time. Sometimes, I feel like Joseph. Sometimes no matter what I do, I have troubles. It's hard to make friends at my new school. I can't find any second graders who will let me sit with them on the bus. When I asked two girls in my class if I could sit with them, they pushed me away.

Teacher: What did you do then?

Lily: I walked away. I went to the back of the bus and asked Cecelia. Nobody likes her either, but I do. She likes to read books about animals, and so do I.

Teacher: I'm glad you met Cecelia. She needed a friend too. So now, your troubles are solved.

Lily: Not exactly. I have two more troubles named Will and Joe. One of them—I don't know which one—tripped me at lunch on Friday. My chocolate milk went everywhere. It was embarrassing. When my teacher talked to Will and Joe, both of them lied about it. Neither one of them would confess to tripping me. I think my teacher thought I was making it up.

Teacher: Troubles, troubles. Just being a student in a new school, you have troubles. Joseph had troubles doing his job too, and I have troubles at work. Sin brings troubles into our lives. Satan tempts people to be mean and uncaring.

Lily: Sometimes, I think I need a super trouble helper.

Teacher: You have one, Lily. It's Jesus. Through His death and resurrection, He conquered sin and death. In His Word and in Baptism, He promises that He is with us.

I have an idea. I'll write today's Bible Words on a piece of paper and put it in your satchel. When you have troubles, you can read about Jesus, your super trouble helper.

Place the note with the Bible Words in Lily's satchel. Set Lily off to the side. Then continue.

Say **Lily had troubles at school. What about you? Do you ever have troubles at school?** Give your students time to share problems. You may want them to break out into small groups or partners. Ask them not to talk about who caused the troubles.

When we have troubles, we wonder what God wants us to do. We might wonder if God wants us to be nice to mean people. That's when we need to think about our super trouble helper, Jesus. God is our strength. God is with us in our sin and troubles and gives us His love that never ends.

For Jesus' sake, God works things out for our good. When troubles come, the devil tempts us to think that God doesn't care about us. That's when we remember that in His Word and in Baptism, God is with us every day. God loves us with a steadfast love. He gives us His care and protection. He provides for us. He delivers us from evil.

Jesus is our super trouble helper. On the cross, Jesus suffered the worst trouble of all, so that we would be delivered from eternal death and could enjoy God's love and presence forever, without end.

Sing "He Cares for Me" (*SGL*, p. 57; CD 12)

Craft Page

To Prepare: Distribute Craft Page 2 (Student Book), glue, stickers (Student Pack), scissors, and key rings and cardstock (optional).

Cut out the backpack and pockets. Students who have difficulty holding paper while cutting may benefit if an edge of the paper is taped to the desk or wall. On each side of the backpack, glue a pocket in place. Glue along the side and bottom edges, leaving the middle and top edge unglued and open. Decorate the backpack with six assorted stickers from the Sticker Page. Write today's Bible Words on the lined paper. Cut them out and slide them into the top of the pocket.

Ask **Where can you put your backpack to remember that God works for you?**

Another option is to cut out the Bible Words on the lined paper and glue them to a piece of cardstock. Cut out the (now sturdy) words again, punch a hole at the edge using a hole puncher, and insert a key ring (or loose-leaf ring) into the hole. Encourage the children to have an adult help them put the ring on a zipper on their satchel or bookbag (backpack), so the attached Bible Words encourage them each day.

4 Closing (5 minutes)

To Prepare: Gather materials to send home.

Gather the children for the Closing. Follow the same routine each week.

Say **God was with Joseph in his troubles.**

Sing "Praise God, from Whom All Blessings Flow" (*LSB* 805; CD 3) or "He Cares for Me" (*SGL*, p. 57; CD 12)

Say **God, the Lord, is my strength.** (Habakkuk 3:19; CD 7)

Challenge Encourage the children to notice others this week who might be going through troubles and to remind them that Jesus is with us and will always love us.

Pray **Dear Jesus, thank You for Your help when troubles come and for Your steadfast love and strength. Amen.**

As the children leave, give them a reminder of God's love.

Say **Because of His steadfast love for you, Christ took your sins, your worst trouble, on Himself. In His Word and in Baptism, He goes with you every day.**

Reflect Generally speaking, 10–15 percent of any school-age population functions with some type of special learning need. Think about the needs of the students in your class.

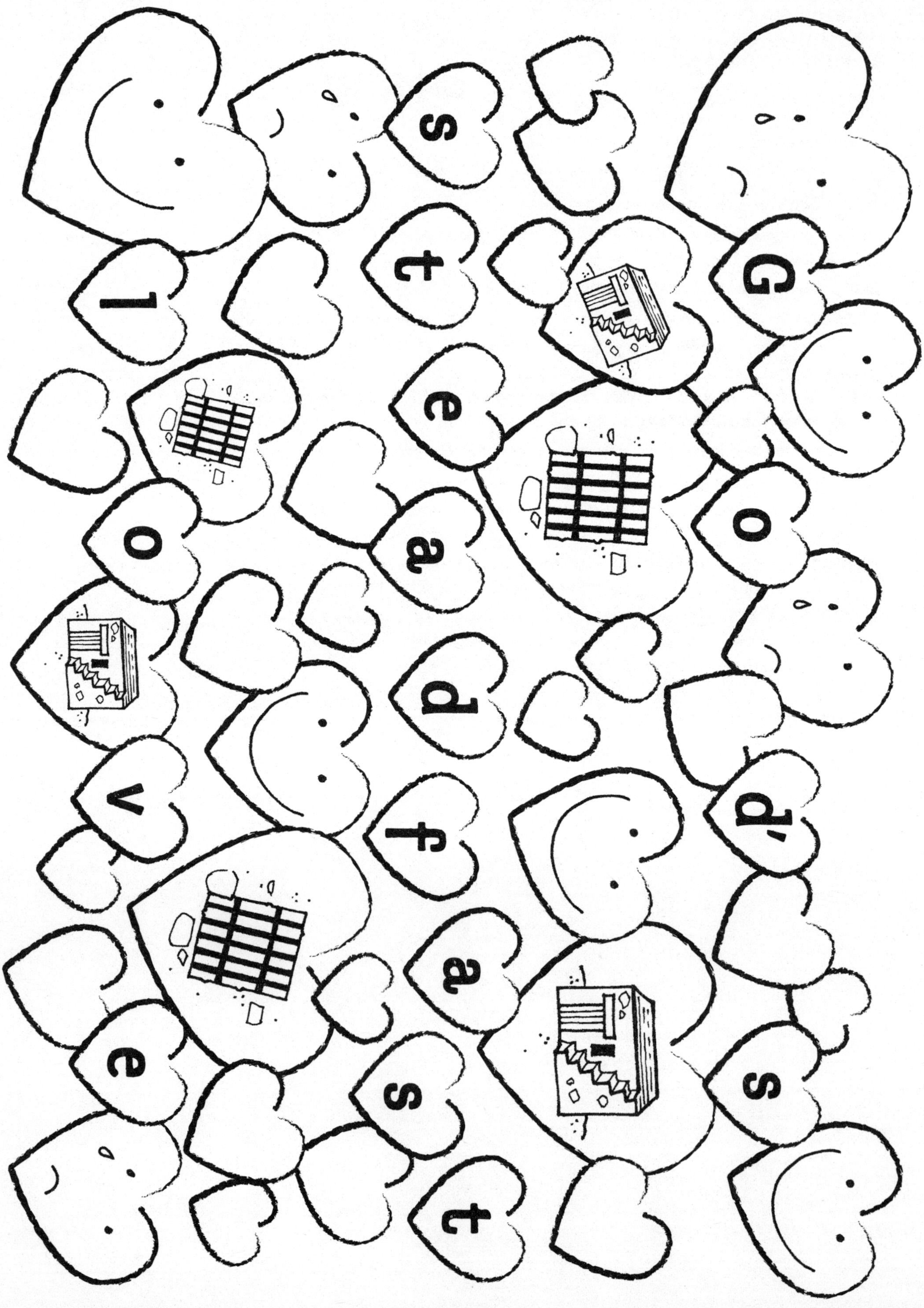

 Activity Page 2 Teacher: This page is also available on the CD in your Teacher Tools.

Lesson 3

Preparing the Lesson

Date of Use

Joseph Feeds Egypt

Genesis 40–41

Key Point

God used Joseph to save His people, all Egypt, and other nations from famine. He sent His Son, Jesus, to save all humanity from sin, death, and the devil.

Law/**Gospel**

My sin causes suffering for me and for my neighbor, and I cannot take care of it. **In His love, God takes care of my needs, both physical and spiritual, forgiving all my sins for the sake of Jesus, who suffered, died, and rose again for me.**

Context

Joseph was thrown into an Egyptian prison after the false accusation of Potiphar's wife. Yet he gained favor in the sight of the prison keeper. God, through the authority of the prison keeper, placed all prisoners under Joseph's authority. The Lord was with Joseph, and whatever he did, the Lord made it prosper.

Commentary

Joseph is an example of patience under the cross. Joseph's exaltation to second in charge of Egypt does not come about without suffering and pain. Only after years of God's forming, planning, and pruning of the rough branches is Joseph finally formed. Just like Abraham, Isaac, and Jacob before him, Joseph trusted the Lord's promises despite every appearance, and he waited for the Lord's time rather than force his own (Psalm 37:5).

God was with Joseph and granted him such outstanding faith. Finally, God comes and liberates him in a wonderful manner, even though Joseph's feet were hurt with fetters and he was laid in irons. Yet, unbelieving Pharaoh raises Joseph out of prison (Psalm 105:18, 20).

God uses the dreamer to interpret the dreams of others. He who dreamed about sheaves of wheat, the sun, the moon, and the stars now discerns the dreams of the butler, the baker, and even of Pharaoh himself. God spoke in visions and dreams and sent Joseph to discern the will and Word of the Lord. God was saving His people Israel through Joseph's hand (Psalm 105:16–17).

God's plan for the salvation of His people required Egypt. No one is as discerning and wise as he to whom God gives the Holy Spirit.

So Pharaoh elevates Joseph to the command of a foreign land. God blesses Pharaoh and his unbelieving nation in order to bless believing Joseph and, through him, all of the children of Israel. The Word and promises of God are sure. The time is coming for Him to call His Son out of Egypt (Matthew 2:15).

To hear an in-depth discussion of this Bible account, visit cph.org/podcast and listen to our Seeds of Faith podcast each week.

Lesson 3

Joseph Feeds Egypt

Genesis 40–41

Connections

Bible Words
The eyes of all look to You, [O Lord,] and You give them their food in due season.
Psalm 145:15

Faith Word
save

Hymn
Praise God, from Whom All Blessings Flow
(*LSB* 805; CD 3)

Catechism
Apostles' Creed: First Article

1 Opening (10 minutes)

Introducing Concepts

To Prepare: Post the attendance chart (Teacher Tools), and set out the stickers (Student Pack) and the offering basket. Have a supply of drawing paper on hand.

Introduce yourself to any new students, helping all students to become acquainted with one another. Record attendance.

Develop the concept that God uses good and wise government as a way to provide food for us to eat. Give each child a piece of paper. Ask students to draw pictures of some of the foods that they ate yesterday. When they are finished, continue.

Ask **Who made it possible for you to eat those foods yesterday? Who bought the foods? Who worked for the money to buy the foods? Who cooked the foods? Who grew the foods? Who transported the foods?** On the board or on chart paper, make a list of answers.

Encourage the children to think beyond their parents to include others who work in fields or factories. Talk about how good government allows for the successful transportation of goods and gives people freedom to order and receive products.

Say **In today's Bible story, God provides food for an entire country, saving people through a special government worker.**

MATERIALS NEEDED

1 Opening	2 God Speaks	3 We Live	4 Closing
Teacher Tools Attendance chart CD **Student Pack** Stickers **Other Supplies** Drawing paper Offering basket Songbook Resource Page 1 (TG)	**Teacher Tools** Poster E CD Glue stick **Student Pack** Stickers Lesson Leaflet 3 Craft Page 3 (optional) **Other Supplies** Resource Page 2 (TG) Activity Page 3A (TG)	**Teacher Tools** Poster F **Student Pack** Craft Page 3 **Other Supplies** Activity Page 3B (TG)	**Teacher Tools** CD **Other Supplies** Songbook

Rituals and Routines

To Prepare: If your class gathers with others for the Opening, begin the lesson with part 2. If you prefer to develop your own opening, a suggested outline follows. For an extended opening, use Resource Page 1 in the back of this guide.

Gathering Song: "He's Got the Whole World in His Hands" (*SGL*, pp. 56–57)

Invocation: **In the name of the Father and of the Son and of the Holy Spirit. Amen.**

Offering

The Commandments: Review the First Commandment (CD 19)

Celebrations: Birthdays and Baptism birthdays

2 God Speaks (20 minutes)

Key Point

God used Joseph to save His people, all Egypt, and other nations from famine. He sent His Son, Jesus, to save all humanity from sin, death, and the devil.

Introducing God's Word

To Prepare: Set out a restickable glue stick (available from cph.org), the Faith Words Poster (Poster E), and the Faith Words cards (Resource Page 2) found in the back of the Teacher Guide. This week, cut out the word *save* from the cards.

The Faith Word *save* can mean to put aside or to rescue. The children are familiar with both meanings. In today's story, God saves both ways. He gives Joseph wisdom to keep, or set aside, food in the good years to use in the bad years. And He rescues the lives of many people, including Joseph's family. Group the children in pairs.

Say **With your friend, think of five things that people like to save.** Give the children time to discuss. **Which of these things are important to save?** After the children finish, continue. **With your friend, think of five jobs in which people work to save other people.** Allow time for the children to discuss their ideas. **In today's Bible story, our Savior God uses a man named Joseph to help people save something that will eventually save them.** Ask one of the children to use the glue stick to add the word *save* to the Faith Words Poster.

Building Relationships!

Telling God's Word

To Prepare: You will need copies of Activity Page 3A and the stickers for Lesson 3 (Student Pack). *Optional:* Craft Page 3 (see page 29).

Play the Bible story on the CD, or read the following script. Ask the children to follow along, placing the stickers where they belong while they listen. In the last part of the story, the children cover the Joseph shown with a sticker of Joseph's new clothes.

Place an open Bible near you. Start the CD. If needed, be prepared to pause the CD recording. Children with language-processing delays benefit from repeated hearings. And some children will listen better with more frequent pauses; if needed, add one sticker at a time instead of waiting until the end of an entire section to add both, as indicated in the script.

Narrator 1: Today's Bible story is "Joseph Feeds Egypt." It is found in chapters 40 and 41 of Genesis. All through Joseph's life, the Lord was with him.

When Joseph was taken as a slave to Egypt, he was a good worker at Potiphar's house. Even when Potiphar's wife lied and Joseph was taken to prison, Joseph was treated well. God blessed his work. While Joseph was in prison, the cupbearer and the baker of the king of Egypt got in trouble with the king. Pharaoh was angry with these two important servants. Guess where Pharaoh sent them.

Narrator 2: To prison!

Narrator 1: Right. The captain of the guard put Joseph in charge of them. One morning, when Joseph came to check on the two men, they both looked worried and sad. Do you know why?

Narrator 2: Each one of them was bothered by a dream.

Narrator 1: Right again. They didn't understand the dreams. They asked Joseph for help. Joseph said that only *God* knows what dreams mean. He asked the two men to tell him about their dreams. The cupbearer went first. In his dream, he saw a vine with three branches. The branches had buds. Later, the buds flowered and ripened into grapes. The cupbearer held Pharaoh's cup, took the grapes, and pressed them into the cup. Then he gave the cup to Pharaoh. What was the meaning of that dream?

Narrator 2: Joseph said that the three branches were three days. In three days, Pharaoh would give the cupbearer back his job. Joseph knew this dream would come true, so he asked the cupbearer to tell Pharaoh about him so that he could get out of prison too.

Narrator 1: That's right. The cupbearer would get his job back. Then Joseph listened to the baker tell about his dream: there were three baskets of cake on his head. In the top basket, there were all kinds of baked foods for Pharaoh, but birds were eating the food out of the basket. What did that dream mean?

Narrator 2: It was not good news. God told Joseph that the three baskets were three days. In three days, Pharaoh would take the baker out of prison to be killed for doing wrong.

Add the stickers to scene 1 at the top of the page.

Narrator 1: Three days later, on Pharaoh's birthday, he had a feast for all his servants. The chief cupbearer got his job back, but the baker was killed, as Joseph had told them. Do you know what happened after that?

Narrator 2: Actually, nothing in our story happened for two years. Poor Joseph. He waited and waited, but no one came to get him out of prison. Even though the cupbearer forgot about Joseph, God did not. He got Joseph out of prison. One night two years later, Pharaoh had dreams that puzzled him.

Narrator 1: Pharaoh was unhappy. He did not know the meaning of his two dreams. He sent for his royal magicians and wise men, but they could not explain the dreams. Finally, the cupbearer remembered Joseph. Do you know what happened next?

Narrator 2: I do. Pharaoh sent for Joseph. Joseph got cleaned up and came before the ruler of Egypt. Pharaoh asked Joseph if he could tell him the meaning of his dreams. Joseph told Pharaoh that *God* is the one who could tell what the dreams meant. Then Joseph listened.

Narrator 1: Yes, Joseph listened as Pharaoh told his dreams. He said, "Seven cows, nice and plump, stood at the banks of the Nile River, eating the tall grass. Then seven other cows came up after them. They were ugly and thin, worse than any cows I have ever seen in Egypt. The seven thin cows ate the seven plump cows. Even after they ate, the ugly cows were still just as skinny and ugly as before. In the second dream, there were seven ears of corn growing on one stalk, full and good. Seven withered ears of corn sprouted after the first ears. The thin ears swallowed up the good ears." Do you know what happened next?

Narrator 2: God told Joseph that the two dreams were about the same thing.

Narrator 1: That's true. Joseph said, "God is telling you what He is going to do. The seven good cows are seven years, and the seven good ears of corn are good years. The seven thin cows and the seven withered ears of corn are also seven years when there will be no food. There will be a famine. First there will be seven years of plenty and then seven years of famine. Since you dreamed it two times, that means it will happen soon."

Now add the stickers to scene 2 in the middle of the page.

"Choose someone who is wise to be in charge of your kingdom. Save food during the seven good years so that the people of Egypt will not starve to death during the years of famine." Do you know whom Pharaoh chose?

Narrator 2: Pharaoh chose Joseph. He gave Joseph fine clothes to wear, a beautiful golden ring, and a special chariot. Joseph was in charge of the plan to save Egypt. All the people were to obey him.

Now, add the sticker to the scene at the bottom of the page. Give Joseph a new coat.

Narrator 1: Yes, Joseph became a wealthy and important ruler. During the seven good years, he made sure big barns were built and wheat was stored. When the seven years of famine started, Joseph opened the barns. He sold grain to the people of Egypt. In fact, people came from faraway countries to buy wheat from him. God used Joseph to save grain and to save His people from famine. God used Joseph to collect food and to rescue His people.

Lesson Leaflet Review

To Prepare: Hand out Lesson Leaflet 3 and a pencil, crayons, or markers to each child.

Have the children review the story by working with a partner to number the scenes in the order in which they happened in the story.

Bible Words

The eyes of all look to You, [O Lord,] and You give them their food in due season. Psalm 145:15

To Prepare: Before class, read through the following section. Sketch out how you will draw the object mentioned.

Draw two big eyes on the board. Below them, draw the other objects.

Ask **Where do your eyes look for food? Do you look in the kitchen pantry or the refrigerator?** Draw a rectangle to represent either. **How do foods get in the refrigerator?** Draw a car and some money. **How do foods get in the grocery store?** Draw a delivery truck. **How do foods get harvested?** Draw a stick person. **How do crops ripen?** Draw a sun and some raindrops. **Who makes it rain? Who makes the sunshine?** Draw a cloud with rays of sunlight. Write the word *God*. **In His love, God takes care of your everyday needs, your need for food, clothing, and shelter. He gives them to us at the right times. God takes care of your need for a Savior. Our eyes look to God for everything we need.**

Say the Bible Words with the children, using the cues in today's Lesson Leaflet as a guide.

3 We Live (20 minutes)

Growing through God's Word

To Prepare: Prepare Poster F (Teacher Tools). Cut apart the two pieces, and make them into a timeline of Joseph's life with a special message on the back. Provide the children with copies of Activity Page 3B (TG).

Say **Sin caused suffering for Joseph. Look at these pictures of Joseph's life.** Show Poster F. **What are some of the problems that Joseph had?** (His brothers hated him. He was sold as a slave. He was thrown into prison because someone lied about him. He was forgotten.) **How did Joseph's brothers sin?** (They were jealous because Joseph got a special coat. They were angry about Joseph's dreams. They lied to their father about Joseph.) **How did Potiphar's wife sin?** (She lied about what Joseph did.)

Sin causes problems for us too. Are people today jealous? (Yes) **Are people today angry?** (Yes) **Do people today lie?** (Yes) Turn over the timeline poster (Poster F). Read the first half of the poster—the Law part: "My sin causes suffering for me and others."

God knew that we were sinners, and He loved us. Read the second half of the message—the Gospel part: "In His love God takes care of all my needs." **Jesus died and rose to save us from something worse than famine. He won the victory over sin, death, and the devil. Through faith, God gives that victory to us, and He takes care of our needs. Let's think about the gift of God's care.**

Ask each child to identify ways that God provides for him or her using Activity Page 3B and crayons or markers. Review the words of the First Article with the children (CD 20), reminding them of God's created gifts ("I believe in God, the Father Almighty, Maker of heaven and earth"). If possible, display the completed Resource Pages.

Craft Page

To Prepare: Hand out Craft Page 3 (Student Book) and scissors.

Guide the children to cut out the puppets and tape the edges to form a pocket for your finger. The children will place their finger into the space that was just formed and then move the figures around to retell the Bible story to their friends. Invite them to use the Lesson Leaflet review as a guide. Consider using a device or several devices to record the children retelling the story. Use social media, the church website, or email to share the video with parents so the story will be reviewed at home. As always, secure parental permission before posting something publicly, or limit access to those you invite.

Say **Use your puppets to tell the story of Joseph, the cupbearer, the baker, and Pharaoh. Don't forget to tell how God has saved you too!**

As an option, use Craft Page 3 instead of Activity Page 3A during the "Telling God's Word" section. Make the finger puppets before the story is told. Let the children move their fingers to interact with one another as they hear described during the story. When the characters are sad, the children can bend their fingers down. Use Activity Page 3A as a review afterward.

4 Closing (5 minutes)

To Prepare: Gather materials to send home.

Gather the children for the Closing. Follow the same routine each week.

Say **God used Joseph to save His people from famine.**

Sing "God Loves Me Dearly" (*LOSP*, page 85; CD 10) or "For Health and Strength and Daily Food" (*SGL*, p. 76)

10

Say **The eyes of all look to You, [O Lord,] and You give them their food in due season** (Psalm 145:15)**.**

Challenge Encourage the children to bring in some nonperishable food items for a collection to a local food pantry. God worked through Joseph to feed others. He can work through them too! Research the needs in your community.

Faith in Action!

Pray **Dear Jesus, my eyes look to You for all things. I thank You especially for being my Savior from sin, death, and the devil. Amen.**

As the children leave, remind them:

Say **God used His Son, Jesus, to save you!**

Reflect Reflect back over today's session. Was there a student who did not participate? Was there a student who lacked confidence? Set a goal for next week. Encourage each student to respond at least once during discussions or activities.

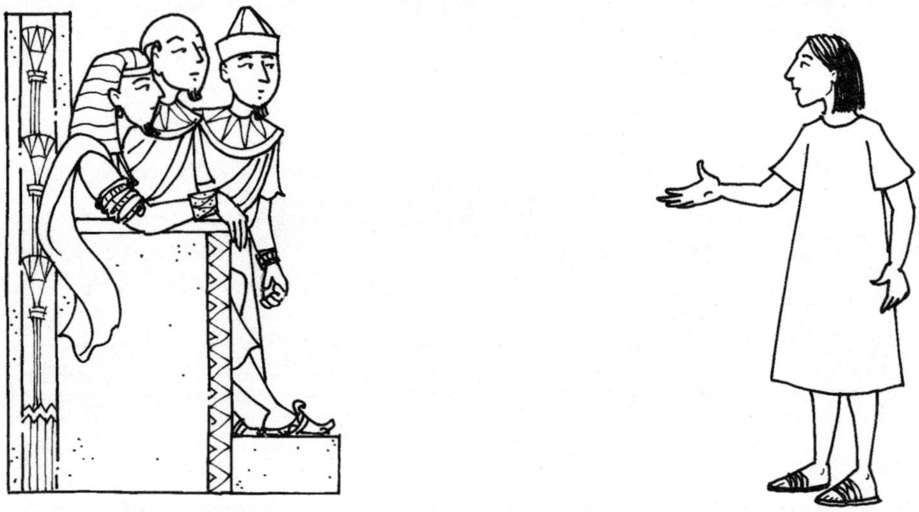

God Cares for Me

Lesson 4

Preparing the Lesson

Date of Use

Joseph Forgives

Genesis 42–45; 50:15–21

Key Point

Joseph revealed himself to his brothers and forgave them. Our Lord Jesus Christ reveals Himself to us and forgives us in His Holy Word and Sacraments.

Law/**Gospel**

The sin I refuse to confess troubles my conscience and separates me from others and from God. **In His mercy, God invites me to confess my sins and promises to forgive them for Jesus' sake.**

Context

Pharaoh made Joseph second only to himself as head over all of Egypt because Joseph was able to discern the dreams God gave him. The seven years of plenty were now over, and the seven years of prophesied famine had begun. The famine was so severe that Jacob's family, who lived in the land of Canaan, felt the effects of the famine and needed grain from Egypt to survive. Jacob sent his ten sons to Egypt for grain; only Benjamin, his beloved, did not go. The ten made the journey to Egypt, fully aware of their sin of selling their brother into slavery.

Commentary

Joseph recognized his brothers, but they did not recognize him. This provides him with an opportunity to bring his family down to Egypt. God used Joseph to save Egypt; now God is saving the family of promise by means of this heathen country. The promise given to Abraham, Isaac, and Jacob is the main focus of this narrative. God promises to give the land of Canaan to Israel. God promises to give Jacob descendants beyond measure. And most important, God promises that the Savior will be born within this family.

The ten brothers are sent to Egypt for grain. Jacob's decision to keep Benjamin at home to prevent him from "some calamity" is altogether human and foolish, as though Benjamin could not die at home, as though his welfare and life were in Jacob's power. If such a patriarch as Jacob, a man provided with great promises, displays such weakness, what courage can we have in dangers and trials?

These things are written to instruct and comfort us (Romans 15:4), in order that we may learn to trust God and work patiently in our God-given vocation. God gives us dangers, trials, and terrors so that we will learn to despair of our own strength and to rely on Him and His promises.

This was also the purpose of Joseph's meeting with his brothers. Joseph acted the way he did toward his brothers not because he wanted them to suffer for their sins, but because he wanted to stir up repentance in them. The terrors and troubles that this caused his brothers were not for Joseph's pleasure or revenge, but for the salvation of their souls. Recognition of sin must precede forgiveness.

Joseph reveals himself to his brothers at the great feast and forgives them, reminding us of how Jesus reveals Himself and forgives us in the divine feast of the Eucharist. Later, after their father dies, he assures them again of his forgiveness, telling them, "You meant evil against me, but God meant it for good, to bring it about that many people should be kept alive" (Genesis 50:20). In all, God's will is done. The brothers repent; Joseph forgives; Israel is saved from famine.

To hear an in-depth discussion of this Bible account, visit cph.org/podcast and listen to our Seeds of Faith podcast each week.

Lesson 4

Joseph Forgives

Genesis 42–45; 50:15–21

Connections

Bible Words

Blessed is the one . . . whose sin is covered. Psalm 32:1

Faith Word

sin

Hymn

Lord Jesus, Think on Me (*LSB* 610; CD 1)

Catechism

Confession and Absolution

Liturgy

Confession and Absolution

1 Opening (10 minutes)

Introducing Concepts

To Prepare: Set out the offering basket, post the attendance chart, and have the stickers (Student Pack) available. In the center of the table, cover a Bible with a cloth. Do not let the children peek under the cloth.

Greet your students as they arrive. Introduce yourself to any new students, and make sure that they are introduced to the other children. Ask the students to place their offerings in the basket and mark their attendance. Then, gather them in a circle.

Say **Something special is before your eyes. Guess what it is.** After the children have had time to guess, ask one child to remove the cloth. **Look. It's a Bible.** Put the cloth back. **Sometimes we can't see something in front of us until someone reveals the information to us. That's what happens in today's Bible story. Something hidden is revealed. Something sinful is forgiven.**

Rituals and Routines

To Prepare: If your class gathers with others for the Opening, begin the lesson with part 2. If you prefer to develop your own opening, a suggested outline follows. For an extended opening, use Resource Page 1 (TG).

Gathering Song: "Forgive Me, God, for Things I Do" (*SGL*, p. 55)

Invocation: **In the name of the Father and of the Son and of the Holy Spirit. Amen.**

MATERIALS NEEDED

1 Opening	2 God Speaks	3 We Live	4 Closing
Teacher Tools Attendance chart CD **Student Pack** Stickers **Other Supplies** Offering basket Songbook Resource Page 1 (TG) Cloth	**Teacher Tools** Poster F Poster B Poster E Glue stick **Student Pack** Lesson Leaflet 4 **Other Supplies** Activity Page 4A (TG) Pennies Resource Page 2 (TG) Cloth Brown paper lunch bags (optional)	**Teacher Tools** Craft Page 4 **Other Supplies** Activity Page 4B (TG) Cloth Plastic bag (optional)	**Teacher Tools** CD **Other Supplies** Songbook *My First Hymnal* (optional)

Offering
The Commandments: Review the First Commandment (CD 19)
Prayers
Celebrations: Birthdays and Baptism birthdays

19

2 God Speaks (20 minutes)

Introducing God's Word

To Prepare: On the board or on paper, write *Canaan* and *Egypt*.

Engaging Activity!

Say **Today's Bible story takes place in two places over several years. One of those places is in the land of Canaan (CANE un), where Jacob's family lived.** Draw stick figures of Jacob and eleven sons near the word *Canaan*. **The other place is in Egypt, where Jacob's son Joseph is now a governor with a very important job.** Draw a stick figure near the word *Egypt*. **As I tell you the Bible story, move your marker from place to place to follow the action.**

Telling God's Word

To Prepare: Give the children copies of Activity Page 4A, and a place marker (penny or other small object). Place an open Bible near you. When you are finished, show Poster B.

Another possibility is to act out the story if you have a large enough class. Assign a child to be Joseph, Simeon, Benjamin, Judah, and Jacob. The rest of the children can be other brothers and Egyptian servants. Use paper lunch bags for the sacks, and consider using a device to record a video of the presentation. Use social media, the church website, or email to share the video with parents so the children can review the story at home or so you can share it with children in your class who are sick or haven't recently attended. As always, secure parental permission before posting something publicly, or limit access to those you invite.

Note: Use Poster F to review the story of Joseph Feeds Egypt.

Where you see an asterisk in the storytelling, pause. The children are to move their markers.

Say **Today's Bible story is from God's Word in the Book of Genesis. It begins when there was a great famine in Canaan, Egypt, and many other places. Jacob sent ten of his sons to Egypt to buy some grain.***

Joseph was in charge of selling grain. Joseph's brothers bowed down to him. Joseph knew they were his brothers, but they did not know it was Joseph. He spoke to them in a rough voice and said, "Where do you come from?"

"From the land of Canaan, to buy food," they answered. Joseph pretended that he did not know them and said that they were spies. The brothers said, "We are twelve brothers, sons of man in Canaan. The youngest is with our father and one brother is gone."

Joseph wondered if his brothers were still mean, since they had sold him as a slave. Joseph said, "I believe in God. If you are honest men, leave one brother here and let the rest go back with grain for your families. Then bring your youngest brother to me. That will show your words are true."

The brothers were sorry that they had treated Joseph so badly many years ago. The brothers said to one another, "We are guilty for selling Joseph. That is why we have this trouble now." They did not know that Joseph could understand what they were saying. Then Joseph turned away from them and cried.

When Joseph stopped crying, he returned to them. So it was that Simeon was tied up and remained behind. Joseph gave orders to fill his brothers' bags with grain and put each man's money back in his sack as well as supplies for the trip home.*

On the way home, one of the brothers opened his sack of grain to feed his donkey and saw that his money was in his sack. He said, "My money has been put back!" This made the brothers very nervous and upset. They thought they would get in big trouble. They said, "What has God done to us?*

When they came home to their father, Jacob, they told him about the ruler in Egypt who kept Simeon and wanted them to bring back their brother Benjamin. Then they emptied their sacks and saw that each man's money was in his sack. Jacob and all of his sons were afraid something awful would happen to Benjamin if he went to Egypt. So Jacob would not allow his sons to take Benjamin with them back to Egypt.*

Time went by, and there was still a famine in Canaan. Finally, Jacob's family had eaten all the food his sons had bought in Egypt. Jacob said to his sons, "Go again and buy food for us."

Judah answered, "We can't go unless our youngest brother is with us. If you will send our brother with us, we will go buy food. If you will not send him, we will not go. Send him with me, and I promise to bring him back safely. If I do not bring him back to you, it will be my fault."

Then Jacob said, "If it must be so, take some of the best fruits from our land and a present of nuts and sweet things for the man. Take double the money. Give back the money that was in your sacks. Maybe it was a mistake. Take your brother Benjamin and go to the man." So the ten brothers went back to Egypt.*

When Joseph saw Benjamin with the other brothers, he told his head servant to make a big feast. The brothers gave the servant their gifts and bowed down. Joseph asked his brothers if Jacob, their father, was alive and well. Then he asked about Benjamin. He said, "Is this the youngest brother you told me about? God be gracious to you, my son!" Then Joseph hurried out of the room, because he started to cry and didn't want the brothers to see.

Joseph invited his brothers to eat in the palace. The brothers were amazed because Benjamin was given five times as much food as the rest of them.

When it was time for the brothers to leave, Joseph had his servants fill the men's sacks with grain and once again put the money back in their sacks. The servants were ordered to put Joseph's silver cup in the youngest man's sack. Of course, the brothers knew nothing about this.

The next morning, after the brothers had gone a short distance, Joseph said to his servant, "Follow the men. When you catch them, ask, 'Why have you repaid evil for good? Why have you stolen my master's cup?'"*

The brothers said, "Why do you say this? We brought back the money that we found in our sacks. How could we steal silver or gold from your master's house? If one of us has it, he shall die. And we will be your servants."

The servant said, "Let the one who has the cup in his sack be my servant, and the rest of you shall be innocent." Then each man quickly opened his sack. The steward looked in each sack, beginning with the eldest. The cup was in Benjamin's sack. The soldiers said that Benjamin must return, but the brothers wouldn't leave Benjamin at a time like this. The brothers were no longer cruel; they could not let Benjamin go back alone. So they all went back to stand before Joseph.*

The brothers bowed down with their faces to the ground. Joseph said to them, "What have you done? Don't you know that I have power to decide whether you live or die?"

Judah said, "What can we do or say? We will all have to be your servants."

But Joseph said, "Only the man who had the cup in his sack shall be my servant. As for you, go in peace to your father."

Judah went closer to Joseph and said, "Please don't be angry with us. You asked us about our father and brother. When we told you about them, you said, 'Bring your brother to me or you will not see me again.'

"Our father said that if something happens to our youngest brother, it would make him sad enough to die. If we return without the boy, our father will die. I promised my father that I would take the blame if anything happened to the boy. Please let me stay as your servant instead."

Then Joseph knew his brothers had changed. They were sorry they had sold him into slavery in Egypt. He told everyone except his brothers to leave the room. He started to cry and told his brothers who he was. He said, "I am Joseph! You sold me here. But it was God's plan to send me here to keep our family alive. Hurry and go to my father. Tell him I am the ruler over all Egypt. Tell him to come and let me take care of our family in Egypt. Don't worry. Now you will have enough to eat." Finally, the eleven brothers went back home.*

When Jacob heard the news, he did not believe it at first. Then when the brothers told him the story, and when he saw the wagons Joseph sent to bring him to Egypt, Jacob knew it was true. He said, "Joseph my son is alive. I will go see him before I die."*

After you have finished telling the story, show the children Poster B.

Lesson Leaflet Review

To Prepare: Hand out Lesson Leaflet 4 and a pencil, crayons, or markers.

Read aloud the sentences from the story. Call on a different child for each answer orally to complete the sentences. Then have the children write the answers on the spaces provided or draw a line to the corresponding riddle.

Bible Words

Great Idea!

Blessed is the one . . . whose sin is covered. Psalm 32:1

To Prepare: Set out a restickable glue stick (available from cph.org), the Faith Words Poster (Poster E), and the Faith Words cards (Resource Page 2) found in the back of the Teacher Guide. This week, cut out the word *sin* from the cards. Cut craft paper into pieces about the size of a recipe card. You will need one for each student and one for yourself.

Say **Sin is breaking God's Law in what we think, say, or do. Let's think of some things that boys and girls do that are wrong, or sinful. Write one of those things on this piece of paper.** Some children may prefer to draw the picture. When the children are finished, draw a pair of eyes on a piece of craft paper. Then invite the children to tell about what they have drawn. **Here are some eyes. They remind us that God sees our sins. Like Joseph, God has power to punish us. We tell God about our sins. This is called Confession. God forgives us because Jesus took the punishment for our sins when He died on the cross and rose again. The work of Jesus covers our sins.** Invite the children to place their "sins" under the cloth covering the Bible.

Now when Jesus looks at us, He doesn't see our sins. Our sins are covered.

Confession, telling God we are sorry for our sins, is a special part of our church service. We tell God we are guilty of all sins, even those we are not aware of. Then we receive Absolution, or forgiveness, from God. Though pastors speak the words, we receive the Absolution as from God Himself. We are blessed with forgiveness. We can rejoice that God is good to us.

13

Sing "I Forgive" (*SGL*, p. 55; CD 13). Use the Bible Words cues to help the children learn the Bible Words.

Key Point

Joseph revealed himself to his brothers and forgave them. Our Lord Jesus Christ reveals Himself to us and forgives us in His Holy Word and Sacraments.

3 We Live (20 minutes)

Growing through God's Word

To Prepare: Cut apart the pictures from Activity Page 4B (TG), and hide them in the Bible that you covered in Introducing Concepts. Cover the Bible with the cloth.

Say **Joseph told his brothers who he was. He revealed his identity. How do you think they felt when they found out their brother—the one they had been mean to—was alive? Now that the brothers knew Joseph was alive, they were worried. After all, Joseph was a powerful man. Do you think they wondered what he would do to them? He had the power to seek revenge and even have them killed. Thankfully, God can restore broken relationships in families. Through Christ, family members can forgive one another.**

I wonder . . . how are we like Joseph's brothers? Remind the children that they have sinned against others. Use specific examples the children wrote down or drew on their paper during the Bible Words activity. **We have sinned against others and against God. Do you wonder how God will treat us?**

We may be tempted to doubt that God loves us. But Jesus took the punishment for our sins. Jesus reveals this Good News to us. Point to the cloth that covers the Bible. **Do you remember what is hidden under this cloth?** (A Bible) **Let's look inside to find the ways that Jesus shows us who He is and what He has done.**

Invite children to search through the Bible for the pictures. Together, read what each picture tells about God's Word and Sacraments.

Say **God is powerful and just. We *do* deserve to be punished for the way we treat others unkindly and for when we get jealous or angry at others. But when God sees us, He sees what Jesus has done to cover our sins. Through Jesus, we are forgiven. We do not get what we deserve.**

Craft Page

To Prepare: Hand out Craft Page 4 (Student Book) and scissors. You may want to provide plastic bags so students can bring the puzzle pieces home.

Help students cut out and put together the two-sided puzzle that emphasizes today's Bible Words.

4 Closing (5 minutes)

To Prepare: Gather materials to send home.

Gather the children for the Closing. Follow the same routine each week. When teaching new songs, use repetition to help new readers learn the words. If possible, place the words on a poster or display them as a presentation using your digital device.

Say **Joseph revealed who he was to his brothers and forgave them.**

Sing "Lord Jesus, Think on Me" (*LSB* 610; CD 1)

Say **Blessed in the one . . . whose sin is covered** (Psalm 32:1).

Challenge Encourage the children to consider this week if there is someone in their family they need to say they are sorry to or someone they need to forgive. You could even show them the order of Confession and Absolution found on pages 32 and 33 of *My First Hymnal* by CPH (order no. 99-2268). Perhaps one of their parents is bitter and unforgiving to another family member. Encourage the children to share hope—God can restore broken relationships!

Pray **Dear Jesus, sometimes I want to hide my sins from You. Give me eyes of faith to see Your love and to experience the joy of Your forgiveness. Amen.**

As the children leave,

Say **Jesus reveals Himself to us and forgives our sin.**

Reflect Children can be introverts or extroverts. Introverts tend to think before they speak. Extroverts tend to think while they speak. Which children in your class are introverts? Which children are extroverts?

Story Map

 Activity Page 4A Teacher: This page is also available on the CD in your Teacher Tools. Growing in Christ® Lower Elementary

Jesus is revealed where His Word is taught.

Jesus is revealed in Baptism.

Through water and Word, Jesus forgives our sin and rescues us from death and the devil and gives to us life eternal.

Jesus is revealed in His Word.

Jesus Christ is the Savior of the world.
He is the key to the true meaning of God's Word.

Jesus is revealed in the Lord's Supper.

Through the bread and wine together with God's Word, Jesus gives believers His body and blood. He forgives sins and gives life everlasting.

Lesson 5

Date of Use

Preparing the Lesson

The Birth of Moses

Exodus 1:1–2:10

Key Point

Through Moses, the Lord saved His people from slavery in Egypt. Through Christ, God saves all people from the bondage of sin and death.

Law/**Gospel**

In this world, I am enslaved by the demands of Satan. **God's Son, Jesus, was born to set me free from the slavery of sin, death, and the devil.**

Context

God declared to Abraham that his descendants would "be sojourners in a land that is not theirs and will be servants there, and they will be afflicted for four hundred years" (Genesis 15:13).

Since Joseph had saved Egypt from famine, four hundred years of bondage to Egypt proved to be God's true prophetic Word for His people. The birth of Moses is the beginning of the fulfillment of God's promise to Abraham that afterward, Israel would "come out with great possessions" (Genesis 15:14).

Commentary

"I'm beat!" We all utter this expression from time to time. It is a simple way to say we are tired, busy, and overwhelmed by the forces of this fallen world and our own sinful flesh. Without relief, we easily become consumed by worry. Our despair at bitter tasks can lead us to unbelief.

Israel was "beat." By the time of Moses' birth, the fruition of God's dire prediction of four hundred years of servitude is evident. God's promise to Abraham of relief must have seemed small and remote compared with the sore backs and calloused hands that bricks, mortar, and forced labor produced. Pharaoh's decree to have all of the sons of Israel killed at birth must have left Israel debilitated in their despair.

Into this world of pessimism, God delivers a son from the house of Levi. Through divine guidance, the midwives defy the death command, and the baby floats downriver to become a son of the household of Pharaoh himself. In this child, the Lord has now provided for His people hope of salvation from their servitude.

Likewise, God declares, "Out of Egypt I called My Son" (Matthew 2:15). In spite of a similar death sentence from Herod, a Hebrew maidservant delivered the Son of God, Jesus Christ. Under the watchful eyes of this new Miriam, Jesus would sail into the hands of the house of pharaoh, the devil himself, where He would suffer the bitterest toil for us. On His back, He would carry the rigors of our servitude to sin all the way to Golgotha. Our Savior would rescue more than the Hebrews. He would free all nations from the bitter toil of our sins and leave the world "beat."

In His Word, Christ breathes healing back into our sin-enslaved souls. In His Word, He proclaims to us, "Come to Me, all who labor and are heavy laden, and I will give you rest" (Matthew 11:28). May we continue to hear the voice of our new and better Moses, the sweet Word of our gentle and lowly Servant, who gives rest for our weary souls.

To hear an in-depth discussion of this Bible account, visit cph.org/podcast and listen to our Seeds of Faith podcast each week.

Lesson 5

The Birth of Moses

Exodus 1:1–2:10

Connections

Bible Words
God is our refuge and strength, a very present help in trouble. Psalm 46:1 (CD 5)

Faith Word
refuge

Hymn
Lord Jesus, Think on Me (*LSB* 610; CD 1)

Catechism
Holy Baptism

1 Opening (10 minutes)

Introducing Concepts

To Prepare: Post the attendance chart (Teacher Tools), provide stickers (Student Pack), and set out the offering basket. Have Lily ready.

Greet your students as they arrive. Introduce yourself to any new students, and make sure that they are introduced to the other children. Ask the students to place their offerings in the basket and mark their attendance. Then gather them in a circle. Take out Lily or another puppet.

Lily enters, panting.

Teacher: Lily, you seem out of breath!

Lily: *(Panting)* Oh, yeah. Sprout and I just finished playing tag. It was hard because we played without a safe base!

Teacher: Really? What's a safe base?

Lily: It's a place where you can rest during the game. When you are there, nobody can tag you. But we didn't have one, so I had to keep running and running and running. Now I'm *really* tired!

Teacher: Well, here's a safe base. You can rest and join us for our lesson.

MATERIALS NEEDED

1 Opening	2 God Speaks	3 We Live	4 Closing
Teacher Tools Attendance chart CD **Student Pack** Stickers **Other Supplies** Offering basket Resource Page 1 (TG) Lily the puppet Songbook	**Teacher Tools** Poster E Glue stick Background B Storytelling Figures **Student Pack** Lesson Leaflet 5 Stickers **Other Supplies** Basket Resource Page 2 (TG) Songbook Activity Page 5A (TG)	**Teacher Tools** Poster G CD **Student Pack** Craft Page 5 Stickers **Other Supplies** Activity Page 5B (TG) Die Cloth (optional)	**Teacher Tools** CD **Other Supplies** Songbook

Rituals and Routines

To Prepare: If your children gather with others for the Opening, begin teaching with part 2. If you prefer to develop your own opening, a suggested outline follows. For an extended opening, use Resource Page 1.

Gathering Song: "God the Father, Bless Us" (*SGL*, p. 33; CD 11)

Invocation: **In the name of the Father and of the Son and of the Holy Spirit. Amen.**

Offering

The Commandments: Review the First Commandment (CD 19)

Prayers

11, 19

2 God Speaks (20 minutes)

Introducing God's Word

To Prepare: Set out a basket, a restickable glue stick (available from cph.org), the Faith Words Poster (Poster E), and the Faith Words cards (Resource Page 2) found in the back of the Teacher Guide. This week, cut out the word *refuge* from the cards.

Set the basket in front of the children.

Ask **What kinds of things might we put in a basket?** Give the students time to share. **Why do we put things in a basket?**

Say **We may put things in a basket to help keep them safe. When fruit is in a basket, the fruit stays in one place. It doesn't roll around and become bruised. When toys are in a basket, they won't get lost or stepped on. Baskets can help to keep things safe.**

Show the Faith Words Poster (Poster E), and introduce today's Faith Word.

Say **This week's Faith Word is *refuge*.** Ask one of the children to add the word *refuge* to the Faith Words Poster.

Lily talked about a safe base. That was a kind of refuge. If they would have played with a safe base, Sprout couldn't catch her there. A refuge is a place that protects us from danger or trouble. In the story today, God uses a basket as a refuge to protect a baby.

Another option is to do a web search for the key word *refuge*. Look at images for shelter in a remote location or a wildlife shelter and discuss how they protect.

Telling God's Word

To Prepare: Set out Table Tent Background B and Storytelling Figures 5-1 through 5-6 (Teacher Tools).

As you place the figures on the background, the children will also act out the story. Have a child who tends to overact during storytelling stand next to you. Your close presence will help that child focus on the story. Before you begin, show the children a Bible. Tell them that today's story comes from a book in the Bible called Exodus.

Say **During the time when the Israelites were slaves to the Egyptians, the ruler, Pharaoh, grew worried that there were so many Israelites. He thought that someday the slaves might decide they did not want to be slaves anymore. To keep this from happening, Pharaoh decided that all of the baby boys should be thrown into the Nile River.** Children can pretend to have an angry, demanding face like Pharaoh.

At this time in history, Moses was born. His mother loved him very much. For three months, she hid him from the soldiers. When she could hide him no longer, she took bulrushes, plants that grew along the river, and wove them into a basket. She kept the water out of the basket by covering it with a black sticky substance that would keep out water. Then she made a bed for her baby. Children can pretend to weave or paint a basket.

Next, she had to do something that was very hard. She put the baby in the basket and placed it in the Nile River among the reeds by the riverbank. Add Figure 5-2 at the river's edge. Children can pretend to place a baby in their imaginary basket. **This baby had a sister. She stood at a distance to see what would happen.** Place Figure 5-3 at the river's edge. Children pretend to peek through the reeds.

Key Point

Through Moses, the Lord saved His people from slavery in Egypt. Through Christ, God saves all people from the bondage of sin and death.

Now the daughter of Pharaoh came down to the river. Her servants walked beside the river. Add Figures 5-4 and 5-5. Children walk in place, pretending they are by the river. **She saw the basket among the reeds and sent her maid to get it.** Add Figure 5-6. **What can be in the basket? she wondered. She opened the basket and saw the baby!** Remove Figures 5-2, 5-6, and 5-5. Add Figure 5-7. Children pretend to draw the baby out of the water and fold back the blanket.

Pharaoh's daughter felt sad for the crying baby. She knew about her father's rule, but she felt sorry for this Israelite baby. Then Miriam, the baby's sister, came out from hiding. Miriam asked if she should find someone to take care of the baby for Pharaoh's daughter. Pharaoh's daughter agreed, and Miriam went to find her mother, the baby's very own mother, to take care of him. Children pretend to rock a baby.

When the baby grew older, he was brought to Pharaoh's daughter to live with the Egyptians. Pharaoh's daughter named him Moses, which means she drew him out of the water.

When Moses was an adult, God used him as a leader of the Israelite people. He would lead many, many people from slavery to freedom. God's Son, Jesus, was also born to set people free. When Jesus was an adult, Jesus saved all people from slavery to sin and death.

Lesson Leaflet Review

To Prepare: Hand out Lesson Leaflet 5 and the stickers for this activity (Student Book).

Discuss the illustration on the leaflet cover by answering the questions provided. Continue with the review.

Children will connect each character to the baby Moses in the center. They will then use stickers to number the characters in order of their appearance in the story.

Optional review: Allow the children to retell the story, using the storytelling figures and Background B. When finished, the children can sing a song such as "God Is So Good" (*SGL*, p. 62; CD 8).

Bible Words

God is our refuge and strength, a very present help in trouble. Psalm 46:1 (CD 5)

To Prepare: Make copies of Activity Page 5A. Have on hand the four stickers that go with Activity Page 5A.

Say **The Bible Words are part of a song written long ago. The words tell us that God keeps us safe from sin troubles and temptation troubles. God is a safe place.**

Say the Bible Words using the cues as a guide. Then pass around a basket. As each child passes the basket, he or she says, "God is our refuge and strength." As each child receives the basket, he or she finishes the Bible Words by saying "a very present help in trouble."

Hand out Activity Page 5A. Children will complete the maze to review the Bible Words for today. They then will add stickers to complete the Bible Words.

Say **God kept baby Moses safe in the basket. God keeps us safe in times of trouble as well. When Moses grew up and became an adult, God used him to save God's people from being slaves to the Egyptians. Through Jesus, God saves all people from being slaves to sin.**

3 We Live (20 minutes)

Growing through God's Word

To Prepare: Set out Poster G (Teacher Tools) and Activity Page 5B (TG). Cut out the safe base cards. You will also need a die.

Say **Moses was saved from death by floating in a basket. Pharaoh's daughter saw him and rescued him. She took Moses into her family. We are saved from sin, death, and the devil by the death and resurrection of Jesus, which are given to us in the waters of Baptism. There, God washed away our sins and makes us members of His Church family.**

But as God's children, we are still tempted to sin, aren't we? It's as if we are slaves to sin and can't stop ourselves or get away from its hold on us. Let's talk about that as we do the following activity. We will think about how Jesus daily frees us from sin and delivers us from temptation.

Children will take turns rolling the die. For each number they roll, they will choose a box on Poster G labeled with that same number to discuss. If they roll a six, they may choose any box they wish. As each box is chosen, talk with the children about why these temptations might be difficult to resist. Talk about how often we give in to temptations. After discussing each box in turn, children will pick up a safe base card and place it on top of the picture. After each play, repeat the following Gospel message.

Say **Through Jesus' death and resurrection, He has freed us from sin and delivered us from temptation. Each day, your sins are washed away and no longer have a hold on you.**

When the game is over, continue.

Say **After he was lifted out of the water by the princess, Moses became part of the royal family. That is true for you too. Through the waters of Baptism, you are part of God's family. You are children of the heavenly Father and members of His family, the Church.**

Sing "Lord Jesus, Think on Me" (*LSB* 610; CD 1) or "Holy Baptism – Part 2" (CD 22)

Craft Page

To Prepare: Use Craft Page 5 (Student Book) and the Bible Words sticker (Sticker Page), along with scissors or tape and glue.

Cut out the baby, the blanket, and the square to make the basket. To make the basket, cut along the diagonal lines of the larger square. After cutting, fold the corner flaps of the large square over each other. Glue or tape down the flaps, making a basket. Place the baby in the basket. The small square will be a blanket. Add the Bible Words sticker wherever desired.

While the children are working, play the CD.

Optional: Use small pieces of fabric for the blanket.

4 Closing (5 minutes)

To Prepare: Use the CD. Gather materials to send home.

Gather the children for the Closing. Follow the same routine each week.

Say **God saved Moses while he was in a basket in the water, and later God used him to save many others.**

Sing "God Loves Me Dearly" (*LOSP*, page 85; CD 10) or "Children of the Heavenly Father" (*SGL*, p. 62)

Say **God is our refuge and strength, a very present help in trouble** (Psalm 46:1; CD 5).

Challenge The princess took a child that wasn't her own into her home. Explain the concept of foster homes. Encourage the children to pray for foster families this week, asking God to bless the relationship between parent(s) and child(ren) with patience, love, and acceptance.

Pray **Dear God, thank You for being my refuge from sin, death, and the devil. Be my help in trouble and my strength in temptation. In Jesus' name I pray. Amen.**

As the children leave,

Say **Jesus saves you through the waters of Baptism.**

Reflect Are you comfortable letting children chat as they work? Learning becomes more solid as children talk through what they have just been taught.

Complete each maze to find the letters of a special word from today's Bible Words. Then add stickers to complete the Bible Words.

 Safe Base Card	 Safe Base Card	 Safe Base Card	 Safe Base Card	 Safe Base Card
 Safe Base Card	 Safe Base Card	 Safe Base Card	 Safe Base Card	 Safe Base Card

Lesson 6

Preparing the Lesson

Date of Use

Moses and the Burning Bush

Exodus 2:11–4:31

Key Point

As God had Moses remove the sandals from his feet, God, in Christ, removes our sins from us, making us fit to approach God and stand in His presence.

Law/**Gospel**

Because of sin, I cannot approach the Lord. **Christ removes my sin so that I am declared blameless before God.**

Context

Moses kills an Egyptian who is beating a Hebrew servant. Moses flees to Midian. In so doing, Moses chooses "rather to be mistreated with the people of God than to enjoy the fleeting pleasures of sin. He considered the reproach of Christ greater wealth than the treasures of Egypt" (Hebrews 11:25–26). In the form of a burning bush, God reveals to Moses that He will deliver Israel into a thorn-free land "flowing with milk and honey" (Exodus 3:8).

Commentary

We all want to be accepted and loved exactly "as we are." God says, "Cursed is the ground because of you; . . . thorns and thistles it shall bring forth for you" (Genesis 3:17–18). On account of our sin, God removes us from His holy presence in His first Eden and clothes our shameful bodies. Our sin, our being "as we are," places us in a more fitting land, where the very ground produces thorns and thistles.

In our accursed land, Moses shepherds his flock. Of all humanity, God might at least accept His chosen Moses just "as he is." Yet God says, "Take your sandals off your feet, for the place on which you are standing is holy ground" (Exodus 3:5). God alone is holy. God abhors anything less in His presence. Moses cannot come "as he is." He must leave behind the reminder of our first clothing and resulting expulsion from Eden, even his sandals.

Nevertheless, who can approach the Lord without downcast eyes? We cannot "as we are." We cannot without God's only Son. Thanks be to God that Jesus Christ has taken the very form of our curse, the thorns and thistles of our cursed ground.

Even more so, the same God who shows Himself to Moses in the burning bush appears again on a new and deadlier tree. Again, He adorns His head in a crown of thorns. On this tree, He removes the effects of the curse from us forever. The thorns and nails of that tree cannot extinguish the burning yet unconsumed light of the world! Indeed, He perseveres even unto death and rises again so that we might know that by His becoming our curse, we are now eternally blessed.

During the Divine Service, we see God loving us because of the thorn-encrusted head of His Son. He beckons us to approach Him and confess our sins, and the great I AM forgives our sins in Absolution on account of Christ's thorn-pierced brow. The Lord removes these sins from us even as He removed Moses' sandals from his feet. In Absolution, God accepts us not "as we are," but for who Jesus is and what He did on Calvary for us. May the Lord continue to direct us to Confession and Absolution so that we may receive the curse-removing love of our Savior, Jesus Christ.

To hear an in-depth discussion of this Bible account, visit cph.org/podcast and listen to our Seeds of Faith podcast each week.

Lesson 6

Moses and the Burning Bush

Exodus 2:11–4:31

Connections

Bible Words
In Your presence there is fullness of joy. Psalm 16:11

Faith Word
presence

Hymn
Lord Jesus, Think on Me (*LSB* 610; CD 1)

Catechism
Apostles' Creed: Second Article

Liturgy
Invocation

1 Opening (10 minutes)

Introducing Concepts

To Prepare: Post the attendance chart, provide stickers, and set out the offering basket. Set out cardboard tubes and tape. Cut strips of red, yellow, and orange tissue paper.

Greet your students as they arrive. Introduce yourself to any new students, and make sure that they are introduced to the other children. Ask the students to place their offerings in the basket and mark their attendance. Then gather them in a circle.

Tell the children that they will be making fire sticks to help tell the Bible story. To make the fire sticks, tape streamers of tissue paper to the end of a cardboard tube.

Ask **Why did people long ago need fire?** Give the students time to share before continuing. **Yes, people needed fire for many things, including light and warmth. They used it to cook their food. In today's Bible story, God uses fire in an important way.**

MATERIALS NEEDED

1 Opening	2 God Speaks	3 We Live	4 Closing
Teacher Tools Attendance chart CD **Student Pack** Stickers **Other Supplies** Offering basket Cardboard tubes Tissue-paper strips Resource Page 1 (TG) Songbook	**Teacher Tools** Poster C Poster E Glue stick Attendance chart **Student Pack** Lesson Leaflet 6 **Other Supplies** Resource Page 2 (TG) Fire sticks Chart of paper (optional)	**Teacher Tools** CD **Student Pack** Craft Page 6 Stickers **Other Supplies** Activity Page 6 (TG)	**Teacher Tools** CD **Other Supplies** Songbook

Rituals and Routines

To Prepare: If your children gather with others for the Opening, begin teaching with part 2 of this lesson. If you prefer to develop your own opening, a suggested outline follows. For an extended opening, use Resource Page 1.

Gathering Song: "Lord Jesus, Think on Me" (*LSB* 610, CD 1)

Invocation: **In the name of the Father and of the Son and of the Holy Spirit. Amen.**

Offering

The Commandments: Review the First Commandment (CD 19)

Prayers

Celebrations: Birthdays and Baptism birthdays

2 God Speaks (20 minutes)

Introducing God's Word

To Prepare: Set out the attendance chart, a restickable glue stick (available from cph.org), the Faith Words Poster (Poster E), and the Faith Words cards (Resource Page 2) found in the back of the Teacher Guide. This week, cut out the word *presence* from the cards.

Say **This week's Faith Word is *presence.* To be present in Sunday School means to be here with all of the rest of us.**

Have the children look again at the attendance chart.

Say **The stickers on the attendance chart show that we are present. God is present too. He is with us in His Word. Hold up a Bible. In today's Bible story from Exodus, we will hear about a time when God showed Moses His presence.**

Ask one of the children to use the glue stick to add the word *presence* to the Faith Words Poster.

Telling God's Word

Engaging Activity!

To Prepare: Have ready a marker or chalk to use on a board or chart of paper. Ask the children to get their fire sticks ready. Set out Poster C (Moses and the Burning Bush).

As you draw the characters on the board (or paper), the children will move their sticks to help tell the story. Place an open Bible near you as you tell the Bible story.

Say **Today's Bible story is found in God's Word in the Book of Exodus.**

When Moses was an adult, he saw his Hebrew people being treated badly by the Egyptians. One of the Hebrew slaves was beaten. Moses was so angry that he killed the Egyptian who had done this. Draw a stick figure with an angry face (use slanted eyebrows).

Then Moses was afraid of what the ruler, Pharaoh, would do to him, so he ran away. Draw an arrow below the stick figure to indicate movement.

Moses went to live in the land of Midian (MID ee un). There, Moses lived with the priest of Midian. He married the priest's daughter, Zipporah (zip POE rah). Erase the board (or use a new piece of paper). Draw a stick person with a happy face with a female stick figure (add long hair) next to him.

Moses spent many years in this land, caring for the flocks of the priest. Add a shepherd staff in the man's hand, and draw a simple sheep.

Once, when Moses was keeping watch over the flock, an angel of the Lord appeared to him in a flame of fire in a bush. Erase the female figure (or tape a new piece of paper over her). Draw a simple bush, but add flames to it. Ask the children to wave their fire sticks around.

Moses looked and saw that the bush was on fire, but it was not burning up. Moses got closer so he could see why the bush was not burning up. Children wave their fire sticks with one hand. They place their other hand above their eyes as if looking closely at something.

When the Lord saw that Moses was looking closer, He said, "Moses, Moses!"

And Moses said, "Here I am."

Then God said, "Do not come near. Take your sandals off your feet, for this is holy ground." Add bare feet (the shape of a foot with toes) to the bottom of the stick person. Children continue waving their fire sticks.

God said, "I am the God of your father, of Abraham, Isaac, and Jacob." Moses hid his face. He was afraid to look at God. Children should cover their faces. **Then the Lord told Moses that He had seen the suffering of His people in Egypt; He had come to take them away from Egypt and into a very special place with good land and good food. He said to Moses, "I want you to go to Pharaoh and bring My people, the children of Israel, out of Egypt." Moses was not sure he could do this job.** Add a question mark near the stick person's head. Children show nervous faces.

God promised to be with Moses, but Moses still didn't think he could do the job. Moses said, "They will not believe me. They will say, 'The Lord did not appear to you.'" But the Lord told Moses to throw his staff on the ground. Erase the staff from the stick person's hand (or cover it with paper). Draw it lying sideways on the ground, at his feet. Children push the flames of their fire sticks inside the tube so the tube becomes a staff. They carefully set their tubes on the ground near their feet, as Moses did with his staff.

Moses threw his staff on the ground, and it became a snake. Erase the shepherd staff. Draw a simple snake. Children wiggle their tubes around.

Then, the Lord told Moses to catch the snake by the tail. When Moses did this, the snake again became a staff. Draw the staff in the stick person's hand again.

Even though the Lord gave Moses many signs, Moses didn't think he was the right man for the job. Finally, God promised Moses that his brother, Aaron, would come to meet him and help Moses with the job of bringing the Israelites out of Egypt. Draw another stick person. Moses and Aaron should be facing each other. Children hold hands with a partner.

Together, Moses and Aaron went to the people of Israel and told them all that had happened. Draw an arrow by the two stick people to indicate movement.

Moses and Aaron showed them God's signs. Then the people believed that God wanted to save them. They bowed their heads and worshiped God. Children bow their heads.

Hold up Poster C. Ask the children if this is the image they had in their minds as the stick figures were drawn. Could they visualize the details? Continue to use the large poster as you move on to the Lesson Leaflet Review and discuss the cover.

Lesson Leaflet Review

To Prepare: Hand out Lesson Leaflet 6 (Student Book).

Discuss the illustration on the leaflet cover by answering the questions provided. Then open the leaflet to the interior pages. Review the Bible story. Read the poem with the children, and discuss the illustrations next to the words.

When reading poetry with children, read it to them once. Then have them read along with you in a rhythmic voice. Or to emphasize the rhyming words, have them read with a partner the second time through. One child can read the first sentence; the other child can read the second sentence (the rhyming couplet).

Bible Words

In Your presence there is fullness of joy. Psalm 16:11

To Prepare: Use the fire sticks along with Lesson Leaflet 6.

As children repeat the Bible Words with you, also do the actions.

Say **In Your presence** *(Shake fire sticks in front of body.)*
there is fullness *(Move fire sticks in a large circle in front of body.)*
of joy. *(Shake fire sticks up high with a smile on your face.)*

We do not need to be afraid that God will punish us for our sins because Jesus already took our punishment on the cross. Because we believe in Jesus, God forgives our sins and makes us holy. Now we can come before God without fear. We can hear His Word. We believe that He is with us in Baptism and in the Lord's Supper. Before God, we can have joy.

You may want to note that at the beginning of the church service, we come before God because the Lord has called, gathered, and enlightened us by His Holy Spirit. In the Invocation, we call upon God to be true to His Word, for where His name is, there He has promised to be. Confession and Absolution follow. At the beginning of the service, our sins are forgiven, and because of Jesus, we are able to approach our holy God.

Share this joy and peace we have—knowing our sins are forgiven and we can approach God—with others! Consider using a device to record a video of the children standing in a row, reciting the Bible Words and doing the actions with their fire sticks. Use social media, the church website, or email to share the video with someone who needs to be reminded that God is with them and brings joy. As always, secure parental permission before posting something publicly, or limit access to those you invite.

Key Point

As God had Moses remove the sandals from his feet, God, in Christ, removes our sins from us, making us fit to approach God and stand in His presence.

3 We Live (20 minutes)

Growing through God's Word

To Prepare: You will need copies of Activity Page 6, stickers for the Activity Page, scissors, glue, and crayons or markers. Before class, check with parents or the church office to find out the dates your students were baptized.

Say **God was with Moses all through his life. You may have heard the story of how God protected baby Moses when he was floating in a basket. Today, we heard how God came to Moses in a burning bush. God was in the bush.**

Ask **God comes to us too. Do you wonder how He comes to you? Does He seem hidden? He comes in His Holy Word and in the Sacraments of Baptism and the Lord's Supper. How many of you listen to God's Word? How many of you are baptized? In His Word and in Baptism, God promises to be in us, in our hearts and lives. Because Jesus takes our sins away, we can be with God.**

In the meaning of the Second Article of the Apostles' Creed, we confess that Jesus has *redeemed* each of us. What does that big word mean? It means that through His death on the cross and His resurrection, Jesus took the punishment of our sin. Jesus made us holy with His precious blood.

As we read God's Word, we find out how God was with Moses. Let's make a timeline to show how God has been with you.

Hand out Activity Page 6. Cut along the dotted lines marked for cutting. Glue the end tabs together, making sure the three strips are in order. Place the baptismal font sticker where it belongs for that child. Add the Bible story book sticker, the Bible sticker, and the church sticker. Ask the children to draw pictures of themselves at different ages. In the empty box, they can draw a picture of themselves in the future. While the children are working, discuss how God makes us fit for service too.

Say **God made Moses fit for service in His kingdom. God gave Moses a task. He also promised to help Moses in special ways. God gave Moses a staff that would become a snake. This staff would be a sign of God's power. God gave Moses a helper. He asked Aaron to work with his brother, Moses. God comforted Moses with the promise to be with him.**

God makes you fit for service in His kingdom. He takes away your sin. He gives you His love and forgiveness in His Word and Baptism. He gives you parents, church workers, and friends to help you in your work. He gives you many ways to serve others. What does God have for you to do today? Where will your shoes go?

God promises to be with you now and in the future too. We could add more pieces to this timeline because God will continue to be with you!

Let the children tell about the kinds of things they could do this week to serve with their hands (e.g., set the table, clean their room, feed the dog) or even with their voice, like Moses (e.g., stand up to a bully, defend a friend, help to lead someone out of temptation).

Craft Page

To Prepare: Hand out Craft Page 6 (Student Book), stickers for Craft Page 6 (Student Pack), scissors, and glue or tape.

Say **God told Moses to remove the sandals from his feet. God put Moses on holy ground. Through Christ's death and resurrection, God puts us on holy ground. He gives us faith. He removes the punishment of our sins from us. Jesus makes us fit for service in God's kingdom. He does this through His Word and through Baptism. One day, you will also receive the forgiveness of sins and life eternal through the Lord's Supper. These are the ways, or means, by which God makes us holy.**

Today, we'll make sandals to remind us that Moses had to remove his sandals in order to approach our holy God and stand in His presence. Through Christ, God removes our sins and makes us fit to come to God, to stand in His presence and serve in His kingdom.

Read together the words on the feet and straps. Cut out the sandals and the straps. Glue or tape the straps onto the bottom of the sandals so that they cross over each other, making an x on the top. The children add the fiery bush sticker on the left sandal and the cross sticker on the right.

While the children are working, they can listen to the CD.

4 Closing (5 minutes)

To Prepare: Use the CD. Gather the materials to send home.

Gather the children for the Closing. Follow the same routine each week.

Say **God made Moses fit to approach Him and then to serve Him.**

Sing "Thank the Lord and Sing His Praise" (*SGL*, p. 41; CD 16) or "Jesus Loves Me, Jesus Loves Me" (*SGL*, p. 49)

Say **In Your presence there is fullness of joy.** (Psalm 16:11)

You may want to ask the children to take off their shoes for the closing challenge and prayer.

Challenge Prepared by God, encourage the children to serve God this week in one of the ways mentioned during the discussion at craft time.

Pray **Dear Jesus, thank You for making me fit to stand in Your presence and to serve in Your kingdom. Amen.**

As the children leave,

Say **Jesus removed our sins from us!**

Reflect Evaluate how the fire stick helped the children understand the story. Explaining in detail the correct way to use a prop heads off the misuse of the object.

God was with me when I was a baby.

God was with me when I was one.

God was with me when I was two.

1 glue tab

God was with me when I was three.

God was with me when I was four.

God was with me when I was five.

2 glue tab

God was with me when I was six.

God was with me when I was seven.

Lesson 7

Date of Use

Preparing the Lesson

Moses and the Plagues

Exodus 5–10

Key Point

Through a series of horrific plagues, God punished the Egyptians for their sinful treatment of God's people and freed His people from bondage. Through His horrific suffering and death on the cross, Jesus takes the punishment for our sin and frees us from sin's bondage.

Law/**Gospel**

On my own, I see no need for God in my life or in the world. **Christ suffered and died on the cross to free me from the bondage of sin, enabling me to see that He is the one I need most in this world.**

Context

Moses returns to Egypt to speak God's words to Pharaoh: "Let My people go" (Exodus 5:1). God inflicts ten plagues upon Egypt, but Pharaoh hardens his heart and refuses to let the Hebrews go.

Commentary

We know our birth dates. We know our favorite sports teams and musicians. We know every desire that can be described as "ours." Yet do we know the Lord God, whose speaking brings about amazing miracles?

Pharaoh does not know the Lord. At the coming of Moses, many gods are vying for legitimacy in Pharaoh's land. After four hundred years of Israel's oppression, the Lord introduces Himself. In the hand of Moses, God's staff-turned-snake devours the staffs of false gods. God's staff turns the waters of Egypt into blood. Frogs, gnats, flies, disease, boils, hail and fire from heaven, locusts, and three days of darkness leave Egypt in shambles. Even with God Himself speaking to Pharaoh, Pharaoh's heart continually hardens to the reality of the Lord's existence.

Without a miracle, our "Pharaoh-flesh" hardens to the reality of the Lord's existence. Astonishingly, God does not content Himself with our desires. God multiplies His signs so His "name may be proclaimed in all the earth" (Exodus 9:16).

"All the earth" is Pharaoh. "All the earth" is us too! God acts to redeem all people. Egypt receives the bloody rivers, famines, and darkened days of God's "wake-up call" so that the Lord might pull all the earth out of unbelief and into knowledge of Him as uniquely God.

In the ten plagues of Egypt, God spoke to His people of old. "But in these last days He has spoken to us by His Son" (Hebrews 1:2). However, God's language is the same. He speaks deliverance for His people through miraculous signs.

As the casting of Aaron's staff causes the plagues of Egypt, so Christ's cross punishes our Disease-bearer for the pestilences of our hardened hearts. As the rivers of Egypt ran red with supernatural blood, so the outpouring of Christ's blood shatters our inward gazing and lifts our eyes to behold the plague of hardness being purged from our hearts. For three hours, Christ suffered utter darkness on Calvary. Thus, the Lord introduces Himself to the world as her Savior. In Christ's cross, we know God as He is. His indefatigable love is for us all.

Through the retelling of Christ's plague-ridden crucifixion, the Lord shatters the walls of our hardened hearts. He produces faith that God not only justly punished our self-idolatry on Calvary, but also loves us so much that He invites us to know Him as He is—pure mercy. This knowledge of God's love in His Son fashions us as His new Israel and brings us from servitude into His heavenly kingdom.

To hear an in-depth discussion of this Bible account, visit cph.org/podcast and listen to our Seeds of Faith podcast each week.

Lesson 7

Moses and the Plagues

Exodus 5–10

Connections

Bible Words

The LORD is my rock and my fortress and my deliverer. Psalm 18:2

Faith Word

deliver

Hymn

Lord Jesus, Think on Me (*LSB* 610; CD 1)

Catechism

First Commandment

1 Opening (10 minutes)

Introducing Concepts

To Prepare: Post the attendance chart, and set out the offering basket and stickers (Student Pack). Have copies of Activity Page 7 and pencils ready.

Greet your students as they arrive. Introduce yourself to any new students, and make sure that they are introduced to the other children. Direct the students to place their offerings in the basket and post their attendance.

Through the opening activity, develop the relationship between masters and slaves.

Say **Let's play a game like Simon Says. We'll call it Master Says. The person in charge is the master, and we are all slaves. We can only do what the master tells us to do when the master says, "Master says."**

To begin the activity, take the role of the master so you can set the tone. Tell the children to pretend to make twenty bricks or to lift a pile of stones from one place to another. Continue with the game as you have time.

Say **In today's Bible story, God hears the prayers of His people who are slaves in Egypt and works to set them free.**

MATERIALS NEEDED

1 Opening	2 God Speaks	3 We Live	4 Closing
Teacher Tools Attendance chart CD **Student Pack** Stickers **Other Supplies** Offering basket Resource Page 1 (TG) Songbook Activity Page 7 (TG)	**Teacher Tools** Poster E Glue stick Background B Storytelling Figures Lesson Leaflet 7(optional) **Student Pack** Lesson Leaflet 7 **Other Supplies** Lily the puppet Resource Page 2 (TG) Water bottles	**Teacher Tools** CD **Student Pack** Craft Page 7 **Other Supplies** Yarn or string	**Teacher Tools** CD **Other Supplies** Songbook

Rituals and Routines

To Prepare: If your children gather with others for the Opening, begin teaching with part 2 of this lesson. If you prefer to develop your own opening, a suggested outline follows. For an extended opening, use Resource Page 1.

Gathering Song: "God Loved the World So that He Gave" (*LSB* 571; CD 9)

Invocation: **In the name of the Father and of the Son and of the Holy Spirit. Amen.**

Offering

The Commandments: Review the First Commandment (CD 19)

Prayers

Celebrations: Birthdays and Baptism birthdays

2 God Speaks (20 minutes)

Introducing God's Word

To Prepare: Place a water bottle in Lily's backpack. Have two or three other water bottles nearby. Set out a restickable glue stick (available from cph.org), the Faith Words Poster (Poster E), and the Faith Words cards (Resource Page 2) found in the back of the Teacher Guide. This week, cut out the word *deliver* from the cards.

Lily: Hey, everybody. Am I glad to see you! I need your help.

Teacher: What can we do for you, Lily?

Lily: I need water to take to my friends. I need to deliver it to them soon because they don't have any. They had a huge storm, and now they have big problems. Mommy and I are going to get my friends and bring them back to our house for a while since it's not safe where they're at now.

Teacher: I think we could help, Lily. (*Help Lily by carrying the extra water bottles.*)

Lily: Thanks. I had better hurry. Bye!

Wave good-bye to Lily and set her aside.

Say **Lily is helping to rescue some people from a big problem. Her story reminds me of some people in today's Bible story. They needed help with a big problem, and they couldn't help themselves. They were slaves who could not get free. They needed someone to deliver them and take them away from slavery. Let's find out how God worked to deliver these slaves and give them freedom.**

Ask one of the children to add the word *deliver* to the Faith Words Poster.

Telling God's Word

To Prepare: Set out Table Tent Background B, the glue stick, and Storytelling Figures 7-2 (Moses), 7-4 (staff), 7-5 (snake), 7-3 (Aaron), and 7-1 through 7-14 (Teacher Tools). You may also want the children to use Leaflet 7 to search for the illustrations that represent the different kinds of plagues (optional). Another option is to look online for an appropriate visual representation of the plagues (e.g., video or slide show).

The children take turns placing the figures on the background as you tell the story. Before you begin, hold up a Bible and tell the children that today's Bible story is from the Book of Exodus.

Say **Moses and Aaron are now in Egypt.** Point to the background. **Here is the palace of Pharaoh along the Nile River. This is where our story begins. The people of Israel were Pharaoh's slaves. They worked hard day after day to make bricks and build him great cities.**

The Lord said to Moses, "Go to Pharaoh. Speak all that I command you. Your brother Aaron shall tell Pharaoh to let the people of Israel go out of his land. But Pharaoh will not listen to you. Then I will use My power and judge them. The Egyptians shall know that I am the Lord." Have a child place Figures 7-1 (Pharaoh), 7-2 (Moses), 7-3 (Aaron), and 7-4 (staff) on the background. Place Pharaoh on the palace steps.

So Moses and Aaron went to Pharaoh. They did just as the Lord commanded. Aaron put down his staff before Pharaoh, and it became a snake. Have a child replace Figure 7-4 (staff) with Figure 7-5 (snake).

Although they did this sign, Pharaoh would not listen to them. Remove Figure 7-5 (snake) and replace it with Figure 7-4 (staff). **So God told Moses to meet Pharaoh at the Nile River and say to him, "Thus says the Lord, 'Now you will know that I am the Lord. Behold, I will hit the water that is in the Nile with my staff, and it shall turn into blood.'"** Ask a child to add Figure 7-6 (blood).

Aaron did as the Lord commanded, but Pharaoh still would not listen. So God told Moses to go to Pharaoh and say, "Thus says the Lord, 'Let My people go. If you refuse to let them go, behold, I will send a plague of frogs through all your country.'" A plague was a terrible kind of suffering that God sent to punish the Egyptians. Have a child replace Figure 7-6 (blood) with Figure 7-7 (frog).

This time, Pharaoh asked Moses to beg the Lord to remove the frogs, but when the Lord did, Pharaoh again would not listen. God told Moses that Aaron should stretch out the staff and strike the dust so it would become gnats. Remove the frog. Have a child place Figure 7-8 (gnat) on the background.

Now little biting flies appeared, but again, Pharaoh would not listen. God told Moses to tell Pharaoh to let His people go. If he would not, the next plague would be flies. Remove the gnat. Have a child place Figure 7-9 (fly) on the background.

So, there came great swarms of flies into the houses of the Egyptians. Still, Pharaoh would not listen. God told Moses again to tell Pharaoh to let His people go. If he would not, there would be a plague sent on the animals of the Egyptians. Remove the fly. Have a child place Figure 7-10 (cow) on the background.

The next day, all of the animals belonging to the Egyptians died. Still, Pharaoh would not let the people go. Plague after plague came. There were boils, or sores, on the skin of the Egyptians. Even Pharaoh had boils. Remove the cow. Add the boils (7-11) over Pharaoh's skin. **A terrible hailstorm ruined the crops in the fields of the Egyptians.** Remove cow. Add the hail (7-12). **There were locusts that ate the plants in the field.** Add the locusts (7-13). **A plague of darkness lasted for three days.** Add the darkness (7-14).

Each time, Pharaoh refused to let God's people go. He refused to listen to God. Through all the dreadful plagues, God was working to deliver His people from slavery. He punished Pharaoh and all of Egypt for the sinful treatment of His people.

Lesson Leaflet Review

To Prepare: Hand out Lesson Leaflet 7 (Student Book) and pencils.

Answer the questions on the leaflet cover. Then open to the interior pages and review the Bible story by searching for the illustrations that represent the different kinds of plagues. The children might also like to retell the Bible story using the storytelling figures.

To foster cooperation with children, join with them in solving behavior problems. If a student has crossed a limit, state the limit. Then teach the behavior you want.

Bible Words

The LORD is my rock and my fortress and my deliverer. Psalm 18:2

Read the Bible Words with the children.

Say **Pharaoh was sinful and didn't think that he needed to listen to God. We are sinful and think the same thing! We don't trust in God above all things. Do we need God?** Allow time for answers. **Yes, we definitely need God. Why do we need Him?** Wait for answers before proceeding. **Yes, we are sinners and need God to rescue us from the punishment of our sin, from death, and from the devil.**

This week's Bible Words remind us that although we are sinful, God has delivered us. Through Jesus' death and resurrection, He has saved us from our sin. He is our deliverer.

Have the children repeat the following actions with you.

Say

The LORD is my rock	*(Make rock with closed fist.)*
and my fortress	*(Place arms in front as if they were a fort.)*
and my deliverer.	*(Push hands away from you.)*

Key Point

Through a series of horrific plagues, God punished the Egyptians for their sinful treatment of God's people and freed His people from bondage. Through His horrific suffering and death on the cross, Jesus takes the punishment for our sin and frees us from sin's bondage.

Great Idea!

3 We Live (20 minutes)

Growing through God's Word

To Prepare: To complete this activity, you will need a ball of yarn or string long enough to go around your entire class.

Say **Today, we will do an activity to remind us that God delivers us from the bondage of our sins. Let's think about sins—things that children or adults do that break God's Commandments. Does anyone have any ideas they'd like to share?** Allow time for children to answer, and share some of your own.

Let's pretend this yarn represents the trouble sin causes for us. I'm going to wrap this yarn around you. Do so. **Even though we don't always see it or feel it, sin entangles us. We are in bondage to sin. A master makes its slave do things. Our sinful self is our master that has us do things against God's will.**

But in fact, at times, we even think we don't need God's forgiveness. We want to do things our own way and don't think we need God's help. We make ourselves like a god, instead of doing as the First Commandment commands: "You shall have no other gods."

Sometimes, we like to forget about the sins that we have done. We start thinking that we don't need forgiveness, but that is a lie. We are sinners and deserve God's anger, just like the Egyptians did. God knew that we needed a deliverer from sin, death, and the devil. Who is our deliverer? As the children answer, cut the yarn that binds them and sing the first stanza of "Lord Jesus, Think on Me" (*LSB* 610; CD 1). **Jesus has saved us from our sins through His suffering and death. Jesus has taken away the punishment of our sin. He frees us to love others and tell them about Jesus.**

Craft Page

To Prepare: Hand out Craft Page 7 (Student Book), along with scissors and glue. Use the CD.

To create the accordion booklet, cut along the solid lines. Then glue the ends of the two pieces together. Fold the strips back and forth on the dotted lines to create an accordion booklet. If you have time, add details to the booklet.

Ask **How are the two sides of our booklet different?** (One side reviews all the plagues. The other side shows us many blessings we receive because of the love of God that comes to us through Jesus.) **We need God. He is the One who provides us with all of these blessings! On our own, we could not take care of our needs.**

While the children are working, play the CD. Spend time with each child talking about the blessings.

Another option is to make the booklet at the beginning of the lesson and let the students use it while you're telling the story during the "Telling God's Word" section. Have the children look at their own pictures in front of them as they follow along.

Option: With the help of the directions on Activity Page 7, show the children how to make an origami frog. Ask the children to tell how God used the frogs to help free His people from slavery. Then ask them to tell how God freed them from the slavery of sin. Remember to send the frogs home so the children can share the story with their family (and challenge someone else to make a frog).

4 Closing (5 minutes)

To Prepare: Use the CD. Gather materials to send home.

Gather the children for the Closing. Each week, follow the same routine.

Say **Through many plagues, God delivered His people and freed them from slavery.**

Sing "God Loves Me Dearly" (LOSP, p. 85; CD 10) or "Jesus Loves Me, Jesus Loves Me" (*SGL*, p. 49)

Say **The Lord is my rock and my fortress and my deliverer** (Psalm 18:2).

Challenge God worked through Moses and Aaron to save His people from slavery. Encourage the children to help friends when they are controlled by sin. Use examples of sin mentioned in the "We Live" section. For example, can they provide a way out when a friend is tempted to talk during the Opening (e.g., not talk back, sit between two talking friends)? Or have the children consider what troubles "plague" the area in which they live. Poverty? Violence? Racial tension (people not getting along)? Is there anything the children can do to alleviate the suffering? Encourage the children to at least pray for those trapped in those situations.

Pray **Dear God, I am sorry for my sins, which bind me. I am thankful that You have set me free. In Jesus' name I pray. Amen.**

As the children leave,

Say **Jesus is your deliverer. Through His death, He has freed you from your sin.**

Reflect Are you comfortable using Lily? To help make reading a script easier, highlight the text in the puppet section. To make it more challenging, use a puppet to represent Lily's cousin, Sprout, who appears on the leaflets. Add dialogue or highlight teacher text in the puppet section that Sprout could say.

Origami Frog

1. 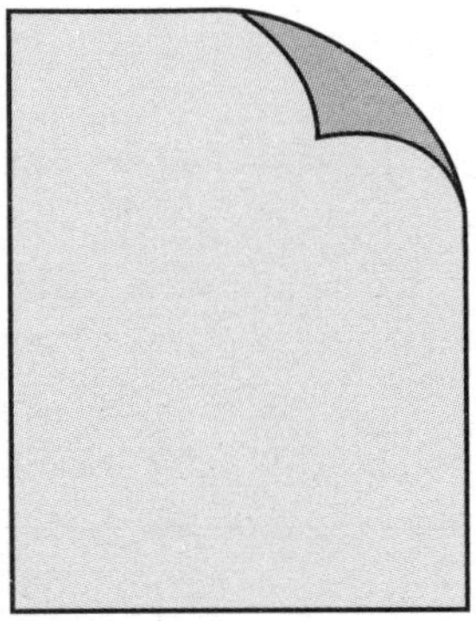

2. 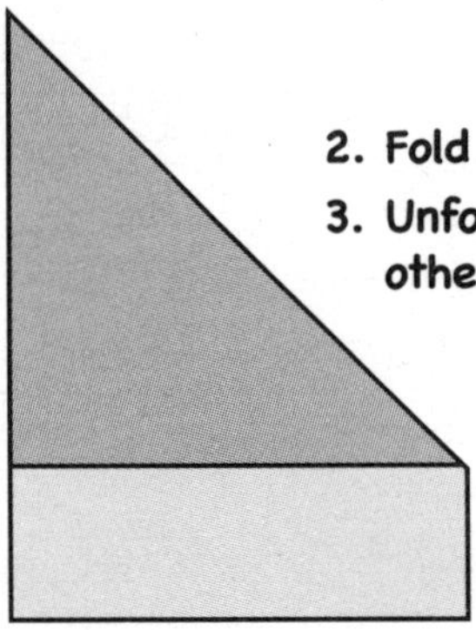

2. Fold along a diagonal line.
3. Unfold and repeat on the other side.

3. 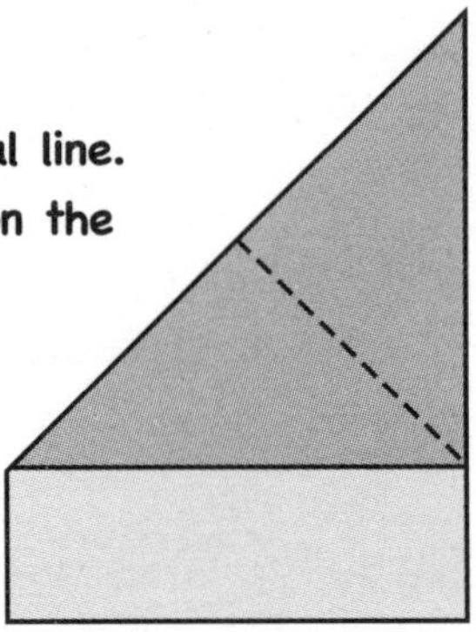

4. Unfold and fold back along the horizontal line.

4. 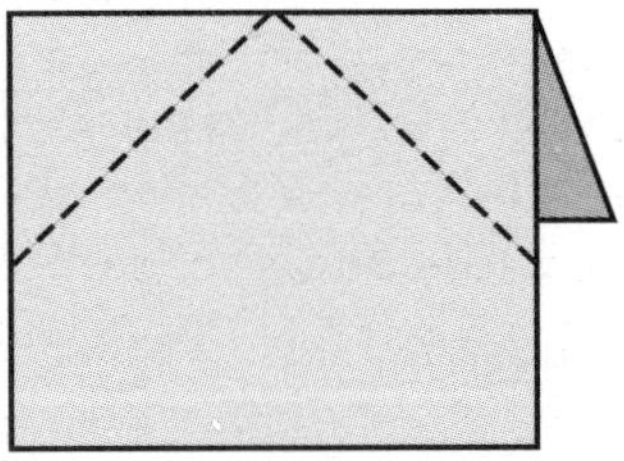

5. 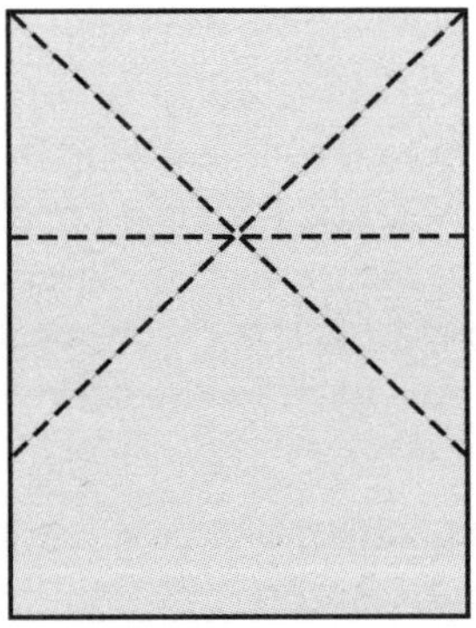

5. Unfold.
6. Carefully fold along the creases to form a "tent."

6. 

7. 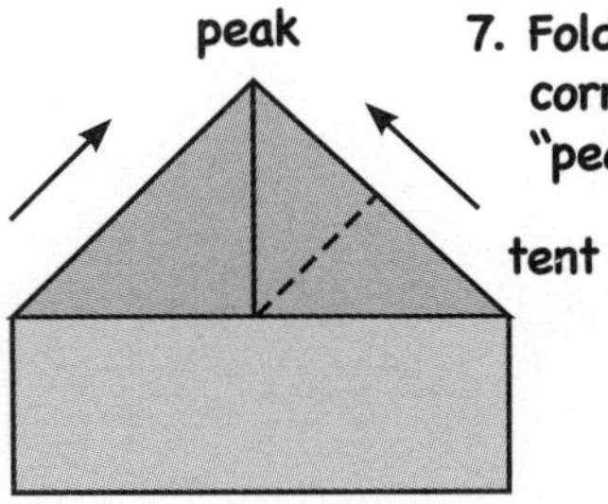

7. Fold the "tent" corners to the "peak."

8. 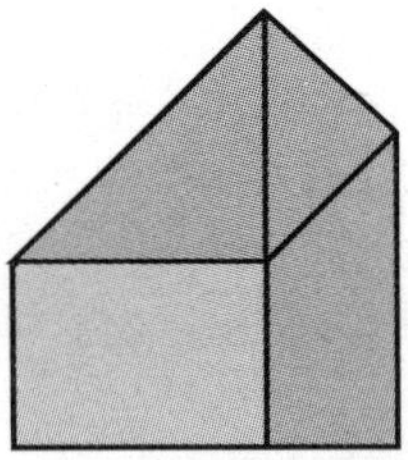

8. Fold the right side over the midline.
9. Fold the left side over the midline.

9. 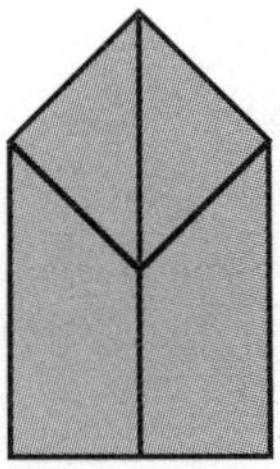

10. 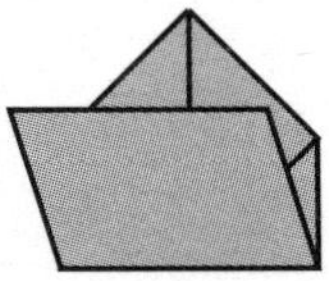

10. Fold the bottom up.

11. 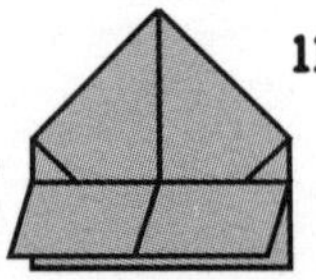

11. Fold down the flap to form hind legs.

12. 

Lesson 8

Date of Use

Preparing the Lesson

The Passover

Exodus 11–12

Key Point

Christ is our Passover Lamb, whose blood was shed for our forgiveness, life, and salvation.

Law/**Gospel**

As a sinner, I fear death. **In Christ, I look forward to eternal life; I no longer have to fear death.**

Context

Pharaoh's continued unbelief unleashes the tenth and final plague on Egypt. God Himself swoops onto the land at midnight and kills the firstborn sons of all Egypt. However, He saves those who, in faith, take hyssop and smear their doorposts in the blood of a male lamb without blemish. The Passover finally causes Pharaoh to let the Hebrews go.

Commentary

God works in mysterious ways. Rationally, we cannot fathom how the sacrificing of a year-old male lamb without blemish can turn back almighty God in His righteous anger. We cannot understand how the blood of a lamb smeared on the doorposts of a house deters death from entering Hebrew households. How can eating this slain lamb bring forth the grace of God in the place of certain death?

Only in faith. Pointing to Jesus, John the Baptizer says to us, "Behold, the Lamb of God, who takes away the sin of the world!" (John 1:29). When our Paschal Lamb drinks from the wine-drenched hyssop branch on the wooden doorposts of His cross, God marks the world as redeemed. God forever ensures that He will now pass over all who look in faith for deliverance from eternal death to His firstborn Son, slain. By Christ's coating of the cross in His holy blood, He destroys the power of death over us and delivers us into everlasting life.

It is no coincidence that Christ institutes His Holy Supper on the day "on which the Passover lamb had to be sacrificed" (Luke 22:7). On this day, Christ takes bread and wine and speaks faith-fathomable reality: "Take, eat; this is My body. . . . Drink of it, all of you, for this is My blood" (Matthew 26:26–28). When we partake of the Supper, we eat the very flesh of the new Passover Lamb. Christ puts His holy blood on the doorposts of our mouths at the altar. Thus, He passes over every reality-denying bit of us and gives us tangible proof of His mercy, for we "taste and see that the Lord is good!" (Psalm 34:8).

In His Supper, Christ causes us to put aside reason and look upon Him in faith. He gives us this faith so that we see Him in true reality, as the Lamb without blemish whose death rescues us from the sin-directed wrath of God. "For Christ, our Passover lamb, has been sacrificed" (1 Corinthians 5:7). May the God of all mercy continue to call us in faith to His altar, so that we may receive the blessings of His sacrificial death in our eating of the flesh of our Paschal Lamb, Jesus Christ.

To hear an in-depth discussion of this Bible account, visit cph.org/podcast and listen to our Seeds of Faith podcast each week.

Lesson 8

The Passover

Exodus 11–12

Connections

Bible Words

[The LORD] passed over the houses of the people of Israel. Exodus 12:27

Faith Word

Passover

Hymn

Lord Jesus, Think on Me (*LSB* 610; CD 1)

Catechism

Apostles' Creed: Second Article

Liturgy

The Sacrament of the Altar

1 Opening (10 minutes)

Introducing Concepts

To Prepare: Post the attendance chart, provide stickers, and set out the offering basket. Set out white construction paper or cardstock, scissors, and markers. Make a sample "Welcome" sign as a model for the children.

Greet your students as they arrive. Introduce yourself to any new students, and make sure that they are introduced to the other children. Direct the students to place their offerings in the basket and post their attendance. Then gather them in a circle.

Say **Sometimes we put special decorations on the front doors of our homes. In December, we might put an evergreen wreath on the door. When we see a wreath on the door during December, what might we think?** Give the children time to answer. **Yes, we think about Christmas. It's a signal to us that the family inside is celebrating Christmas. What decorations might you put out to celebrate the coming of spring?** (Spring flowers in a wreath or a basket) **What would you use on your door if you wanted to signal whose home it was?** (Put the first letter of your last name on the door) **Today, we'll be making a welcome sign to place on the door. It will be a signal to others, showing that we are happy to have someone come to our home.**

Hand out a piece of white construction paper or cardstock. Write the word "Welcome" on the board and give the children time to copy the letters onto their paper using large letters that take up most of the page; show an example.

MATERIALS NEEDED

1 Opening	2 God Speaks	3 We Live	4 Closing
Teacher Tools Attendance chart CD **Student Pack** Stickers **Other Supplies** Offering basket Resource Page 1 (TG) White construction paper or cardstock Songbook	**Teacher Tools** Poster E Glue stick Poster D **Student Pack** Lesson Leaflet 10 Sticker **Other Supplies** Resource Page 2 (TG) Activity Page 8A (TG) Activity Page 8B (TG)	**Teacher Tools** CD **Student Pack** Craft Page 8 Stickers **Other Supplies** Activity Page 8A Construction paper Yarn Songbook	**Teacher Tools** CD **Other Supplies** Songbook

Encourage them to decorate the letters and to add their own border or cut the outer edges of the welcome sign in a design (e.g., make rounded edges, clip the corners, make scalloped edges, snip the edges).

Another option would be to use publishing software or a digital product that helps students design a sign to save and print. If you have a limited number of devices, have the children work together in small groups or as a class to design a welcome sign.

Take note of any children who may mention something about a family member not being welcome in their home; be alert to any situations where members of the family are struggling to communicate in a healthy way, and pray for God to make their home a loving, safe, welcoming place to enter.

Rituals and Routines

To Prepare: If your children gather with others for the Opening, begin teaching with part 2. If you prefer to develop your own opening, a suggested outline follows. For an extended opening, use Resource Page 1.

Gathering Song: "Praise and Thanksgiving" (*SGL*, p. 39; CD 15)

Invocation: **In the name of the Father and of the Son and of the Holy Spirit. Amen.**

Offering

The Commandments: Review the First Commandment (CD 19)

Prayers

Celebrations: Birthdays and Baptism birthdays

15, 19

2 God Speaks (20 minutes)

Introducing God's Word

To Prepare: Set out paper, markers or crayons, a restickable glue stick (available from cph.org), the Faith Words Poster (Poster E), and the Faith Words cards (Resource Page 2) found in the back of the Teacher Guide. This week, cut out the word *Passover* from the cards.

Group the children in pairs, and give each pair paper and markers or crayons. Ask the pairs to think of as many holidays as they can.

Say **With your friend, think of as many holidays as you can. On your paper, draw a picture or write a word about the holiday that will help you remember each one.** Give the children a few minutes to work. After a while, give the pairs a chance to share their lists with one another. When they have finished, continue.

Say **Some holidays remind us of festivals we celebrate during the Church Year. Which holidays would those be?** (Christmas and Easter)

If you were Jewish and living in Jesus' day, you might have thought of Passover as a holiday. Passover was celebrated each year to remember one special night. It was a night when God's angel of death passed over the homes that were marked in a special way. It was a night when God's

people became free. It was a night when God's people were saved. It was the night of Passover.

Ask one of the children to add the word *Passover* to the Faith Words Poster.

Telling God's Word

To Prepare: Set out Poster D. Make copies of pieces A–D from Activity Page 8B (TG). Also make copies of Activity Page 8A (TG) for each child. Each child will need scissors and a red crayon or marker.

Each child needs to cut out the four pieces from Activity Page 8B, cut open the door of Activity Page 8A, and cut out the window of Activity Page 8A.

Before you begin, show the children a Bible, and tell them that the story you are telling comes from the Book of Exodus. Place the open Bible near you.

Say **As I tell today's Bible story, we will look carefully at this poster. We will also use our crayon and the cutout pieces with Activity Page 8A.**

God wanted to free His people from slavery in Egypt. He wanted to take them to a new land. He sent Moses and his brother, Aaron, to talk to Pharaoh, the ruler of Egypt. Pharaoh would not obey God, so many bad things happened to the people of Egypt.

Do you know any of those bad things that happened? The bad things were called plagues. Let the children tell. **After nine plagues, Pharaoh refused to let Moses and God's people leave Egypt. Finally, the Lord said to Moses, "I will bring one more plague upon Pharaoh and upon Egypt. Afterward, Pharaoh will let My people go."**

So Moses said to God's people, "Thus says the Lord: 'About midnight I will send an angel to every family in Egypt. During that night, the oldest boy in every family in Egypt will die. There shall be a great cry throughout all the land of Egypt.'"

Direct the children to look closely at the faces of the Israelites on Poster D. **Here are some of God's people, the Israelites. Do they look frightened?** Allow time for answers.

Although what God said was very scary, the Israelites trusted God. God had given them faith to believe He would save them. Through Moses, God told the Israelites that each family should take a lamb and kill it. Then they should take some of the blood of the lamb and put it on the doorposts—on the sides of the doors and the top of the doors. Point to the poster. **See what this boy and his father are doing.**

Ask the students to take the hyssop branch (A) and brush the doorframe of Activity Page 8A. Tell them to imagine they are brushing the doorposts with the blood of the lamb. They may use a red crayon or marker to make it look more realistic.

Say **Through Moses, God told the Israelites to eat quickly. He even told them what to eat. They were to eat roasted lamb with unleavened, or flat, bread and bitter herbs.** Have the children pretend to eat their meal in a hurry. **He told them to dress in traveling clothes, with their belts fastened, sandals on, and staff ready.**

Ask the students to look at the two girls and their mother on Poster D. Ask them to place pieces B, C, and D through the cutout window of Activity Page 8A. This is the Passover table.

Say **God told Moses to tell all the people that this last plague would be the Lord's Passover. God said He would send an angel to kill the oldest son in every home. The only people who would not suffer and would not need to fear death would be those whose houses had the blood of the lamb on them. The angel would pass over those homes.**

It all happened just as God had said. At midnight, the oldest son in every family in the land of Egypt died. The people of Egypt cried bitter tears. Every family had lost someone.

Finally, after the last terrible plague, Pharaoh let God's people go. That night, he called Moses and Aaron and said, "Go, both of you and the people of Israel. Serve the Lord, as you have said."

When the Israelites heard all that God had done to save them, what do you think they did? The Bible says that they bowed their heads and worshiped God.

Ask each child to write his or her name on Activity Page 8A. Collect them for later use.

Lesson Leaflet Review

To Prepare: Hand out Lesson Leaflet 8 and the stickers for this lesson.

Discuss the illustration on the leaflet cover by answering the questions provided. Then open the leaflet to the interior pages to review the Bible story. Children will read about what God told Moses He would do and what God told the Israelites to do. As they read each sentence, they will check it off by placing a sticker near the sentence.

Option: Allow the children to retell the story themselves by using pieces A–D from Activity Page 8B. When they have finished, the children can sing a song of thanksgiving, such as "Thank the Lord and Sing His Praise" (*SGL*, p. 41; CD 16).

16

Bible Words

[The Lord] passed over the houses of the people of Israel. Exodus 12:27

Say **God had mercy on His people. He passed over the houses of the Israelites, and they were not harmed. Let's learn the Bible Words for today so that we can better remember that God has mercy on us.**

Have the children repeat the following actions with the Bible Words.

Say

[The Lord] passed over	*(Move hands as if passing over something.)*
the houses	*(Make a point with your hands together in front of you.)*
of the people of Israel.	*(Join hands with classmates.)*

3 We Live (20 minutes)

Key Point

Christ is our Passover Lamb, whose blood was shed for our forgiveness, life, and salvation.

Growing through God's Word

To Prepare: Be prepared to distribute Activity Page 8A again. You will also need construction paper, tape, and the stickers (Student Pack).

Say **It's hard to believe that the Israelites really needed to kill a lamb to live. It's hard to believe that in the last and worst plague, they needed the blood of a lamb to make sure that the angel would pass over their homes. But it was true. Without that blood, each family would have experienced death. But with that blood on the sides of the door and on the top of the door, each family was free from death and free from their lives as slaves.**

Let's think about our lives as slaves. Did you know that you were born as a slave to sin? It's difficult to believe that Jesus needed to die on the cross so that we could be free. But it's true. Only Jesus' blood shed on a cross could get rid of our awful and ugly sin. Jesus, the Lamb of God, died so that our sins could be forgiven. Even though our sin is awful and ugly, God's love is far greater than sin.

We confess our faith in Jesus as our Lamb of God in the words of the Apostles' Creed. Jesus Christ "was crucified, died and was buried. He descended into hell. The third day He rose again from the dead." Jesus freed me from all sins, from death, and from the power of the devil.

Great Idea!

Tape the construction paper to the back of Activity Page 8A, keeping the door free to open and close. Place the Lamb of God sticker on the top of the doorpost and the crucifix sticker inside the door.

Say **Instead of celebrating Passover, Christians celebrate the Sacrament of the Altar. We also call this meal the Lord's Supper. Before going to the Lord's Supper, we sing, "Lamb of God, You take away the sin of the world; have mercy on us." In the Lord's Supper, believers receive the forgiveness of sins and life everlasting. In, with, and under the bread and wine, God gives believers the very body and blood of Jesus. Because of Jesus' blood shed on the cross, we don't need to be afraid of death.**

Ask the children to add the sticker representing the Lord's Supper inside the window.

Say **When we realize what God has done for us, we can also bow our heads and worship Him.**

Close this section by singing or praying "Lamb of God, You Take Away" (*SGL*, p. 52) or "Lord Jesus, Think on Me" (*LSB* 610; CD 1).

Craft Page

To Prepare: Hand out Craft Page 8 (Student Book), along with scissors, tape, and pieces of yarn.

Cut out the two rectangles, and roll them into tube shapes. Tape the edges to secure them. Cut out the Lamb of God symbol. Tape the shorter tube to the longer tube, creating a cross. Tape the symbol of Christ as the victorious lamb to the middle of the cross, where the tubes meet. Tape a loop of yarn to the back of each cross so that it can be hung. If children have difficulty taping things together, have them work in pairs. One person holds the project while the other person tapes.

While the children are working, play the CD. When they have finished,

Say **Hang this cross in your home to remind your family that all of your blessings, including heaven, come to you because of Jesus, your Savior. Because of Jesus, the Lamb of God, you don't need to be afraid of death. Our home is in heaven. Jesus will welcome us with open arms and will tell us "Come!"**

4 Closing (5 minutes)

To Prepare: Gather Lesson Leaflets, storytelling materials, and the craft to send home.

Gather the children for the Closing. Follow the same routine each week.

Say **Long ago, God's people were saved from death and set free by the blood of a lamb.**

Sing "Lamb of God, You Take Away" (*SGL*, p. 52)

Say **[The Lord] passed over the houses of the people of Israel** (Exodus 12:27).

Challenge Encourage the children to use their creativity to "decorate" the doors of homes in their neighborhood. Can they hang a May Day basket? Can they share a thank-you card for the neighbor's beautiful flowers or enjoyable Christmas decorations? What else would be appropriate? Remind them to include a Bible verse too, so they share words of life.

Faith in Action!

Pray **Dear Jesus, thank You for shedding Your blood on the cross so that I might be free from sin, death, and the devil. Amen.**

As the children leave,

Say **Jesus, the Lamb of God, saved you.**

Reflect Do you allow your students to be creative? When allowed to personalize projects, children experience more ownership and build insights.

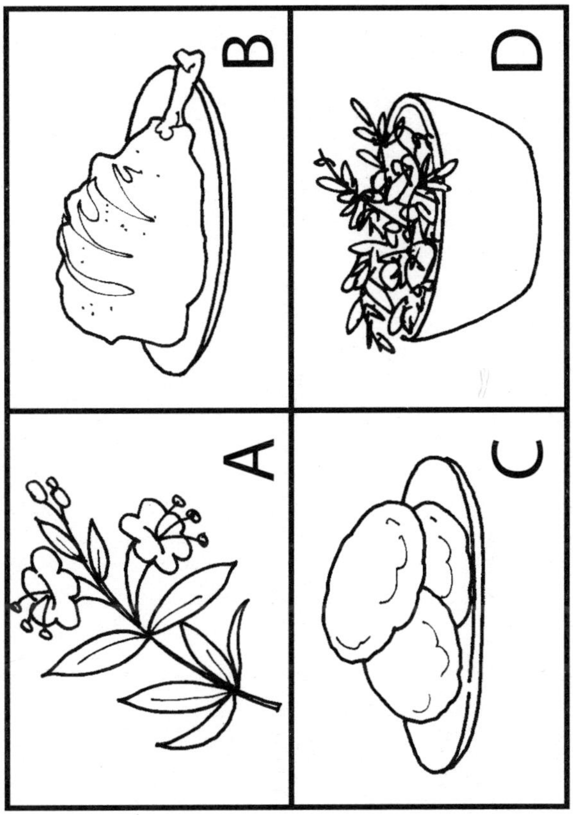

Activity Page 8B. Teacher: This page is also available on the CD in your Teacher Tools.

Lesson 9

Preparing the Lesson

Date of Use

Crossing the Red Sea

Exodus 13:17–15:21

Key Point

As God saved the Hebrews through the water of the Red Sea, He saves us through the washing of water in Holy Baptism, conquering Satan, our greatest enemy.

Law/**Gospel**

The waves of this sinful world surge around me and drain me of life. **The waters of Holy Baptism wash me clean of sin and grant me life eternal.**

Context

Pharaoh lets the Hebrews go, but he soon regrets having done so. Pharaoh unleashes his unholy host upon the hapless Hebrews and quickly overtakes them. God fights for His people as a pillar of cloud and fire. In the hand of Moses, God's staff parts the Red Sea, thereby giving dry ground so the children of Israel might cross. Afterward, God topples the watery walls of the sea and destroys the very army bent on the destruction of His people.

Commentary

Hopeless! Perhaps we feel hopeless at times. We see no way out of our situations. Our sins, this world, even the devil and his minions envelop our entire view and obscure all hope.

The Israelites feel hopeless. All the wanting in the world cannot give them the power to defeat the mighty armies seeking to subjugate them again. Likewise, wave after wave of watery death stands before them. Fearing the circumstances, they respond naturally by grumbling: "Is it because there are no graves in Egypt that you have taken us away to die in the wilderness?" (Exodus 14:11). Whereas our eyes see only death by sword or water, God speaks salvation: "Fear not, stand firm, and see the salvation of the Lord" (Exodus 14:13). Thus, the water parts, providing a pathway to paradise for God's people.

This salvation for the children of Israel in the crossing of the Red Sea foreshadows the watery deliverance of the new Israel. Thus, "all were baptized into Moses in the cloud and in the sea" (1 Corinthians 10:2). Likewise, in the Red Sea of Christ's crucifixion, Christ's blood purges the demonic death grip that the devil has on God's creation. On Calvary, Christ takes the worst that this world can dish out and bears the marks of our sinful complaints on His beaten and bloodied body.

Thus, Christ restores hope for us. God gives this hope to us in His same watery way. In our Baptism, we "stand firm, and see the salvation of the Lord." God tinges crimson our Red Sea baptismal fonts by the blood of His Son. In our consecrated baptismal waters, God washes away our sinful griping and the pursuing Egyptian demons.

From font to funeral, God continually fills us with His hope because He drenched us by His "washing of regeneration and renewal of the Holy Spirit" (Titus 3:5). We are never hopeless because God promises to fight for us. "Let us draw near . . . with our hearts sprinkled clean from an evil conscience and our bodies washed with pure water. Let us hold fast the confession of our hope without wavering, for He who promised is faithful" (Hebrews 10:22–23).

To hear an in-depth discussion of this Bible account, visit cph.org/podcast and listen to our Seeds of Faith podcast each week.

Lesson 9

Crossing the Red Sea

Exodus 13:17–15:21

Connections

Bible Words

Fear not, stand firm, and see the salvation of the LORD. Exodus 14:13

Faith Word

salvation

Hymn

O Sing to the Lord (*LSB* 808; CD 2)

Catechism

Holy Baptism

1 Opening (10 minutes)

Introducing Concepts

To Prepare: Post the attendance chart. Set out the stickers (Student Pack) and the offering basket. Provide copies of Activity Page 9A and the bridge sticker (Student Pack). Consider using a device to record the children working together during the Opening and posting the video on your church website. What a great example of how students interact with one another and learn important biblical truths during Sunday School! As always, secure parental permission before posting something publicly, or limit access to those you invite.

Greet your students as they arrive. Introduce yourself to any new students, and make sure that they are introduced to the other children. Direct the students to place their offerings in the basket and post their attendance.

Gather the children to work in pairs, giving them copies of Activity Page 9A. Give out the bridge stickers later.

Building Relationships!

Say **When we have problems, we often feel bad. The problems are like roadblocks. They keep us from getting our way or from getting something we want. Some of the problems are little, while others seem big and overwhelming. Work with your partner to find a way through the maze of problems on Activity Page 9A.**

Give the children time to work together. Note that it will be impossible for the children to find a way through the maze without the sticker that you will give to them. Once you see that the children cannot make it through, ask them to share with you what is wrong. Then give them the bridge sticker. When they have completed the maze, continue.

MATERIALS NEEDED

1 Opening	2 God Speaks	3 We Live	4 Closing
Teacher Tools Attendance chart CD **Student Pack** Stickers **Other Supplies** Offering basket Activity Page 9A (TG) Resource Page 1 (TG) Songbook	**Teacher Tools** Poster E Glue stick CD **Student Pack** Lesson Leaflet 9 **Other Supplies** Resource Page 2 (TG) Blue streamers Craft Page 9 (optional) Cut straws (optional)	**Teacher Tools** CD **Student Pack** Craft Page 9 **Other Supplies** 4 signs Activity Page 9B (TG) Cut straws Construction paper	**Teacher Tools** CD **Other Supplies** Songbook

Say **You did it, but you needed me to rescue you. You needed my help to escape. In today's story, the people of God need a rescue too. As you listen to the Bible story, find out about God's escape plan and rescue.**

Rituals and Routines

To Prepare: If your children gather with others for the Opening, begin teaching with part 2. If you prefer to develop your own opening, a suggested outline follows. For an extended opening, use Resource Page 1.

Gathering Song: "Praise and Thanksgiving" (*SGL*, p. 39; CD 15)

Invocation: **In the name of the Father and of the Son and of the Holy Spirit. Amen.**

Offering

The Commandments: Review the First Commandment (CD 19)

Prayers

Celebrations: Birthdays and Baptism birthdays

2 God Speaks (20 minutes)

Introducing God's Word

To Prepare: Set out a restickable glue stick (available from cph.org), the Faith Words Poster (Poster E), and the Faith Words cards (Resource Page 2) found in the back of the Teacher Guide. This week, cut out the word *salvation* from the cards.

Show the Faith Words Poster (Poster E).

Say **I'm thinking of a word that means an escape or a rescue. To help you understand this word, pretend that you are trapped inside a deep hole. You cannot find your way out. You have no food or water. Hours pass, and no help comes your way. You scream for help until you are so tired that you sit down. Finally, after you have given up, someone comes to help. The person gives you a rope and pulls you out. The person give you food and water. He or she rescues you and helps you escape.**

The person who threw you the rope saved you. What you experienced was . . . salvation.

Ask one of the children to use the glue stick to add the word *salvation* on Poster E.

In today's Bible story, God's people are trapped. They need an escape. They need a rescue. Let's listen to the Bible story and find out what happens to them and how God works out their salvation.

Telling God's Word

To Prepare: Cut two blue streamers of tissue paper, ribbon, or fabric strips about two feet long for each child. Review the CD storytelling before class. Have the CD and Bible ready. Before class, you may want the children to use Craft Page 9 to make the puppets to use during the storytelling (optional).

Active Learning Idea!

Hold up a Bible. Tell the children that the story comes from the Book of Exodus in the Bible. Place the open Bible near you. Organize the children in two rows, facing each other. Each child has two streamers. Remember to explain in detail how you would like the children to handle props such as streamers before you begin using them.

Say **As we listen to today's Bible story on the CD, follow the directions. Move your streamers the way I move mine. Our blue streamers represent a body of water called the Red Sea.**

Narrator 1: Move the streamers back and forth in front of you from left to right.

After the last and worst plague, Pharaoh let the Israelite slaves go. God led them away from Egypt, toward the Red Sea. The Lord went before them in a pillar of cloud by day and a pillar of fire by night. At first, Pharaoh was eager to be rid of the Israelites and the terrible plagues of their God. However, Pharaoh quickly changed his mind. If you were there, you might have heard Pharaoh say:

Narrator 2: What have I done? Why did I let those Israelite slaves go?

Narrator 1: Soon, Pharaoh got his chariot and army ready. He took six hundred of his best chariots and all the other chariots of Egypt with officers over all of them. The Egyptians chased after the Israelites and came near them when they were camped by the Red Sea. When the Israelites saw the chariots coming after them, they were afraid. There was no way out. If you were there, you might have heard them complain and ask:

Narrator 2: Moses, what have you done to us? It would have been better for us to serve the Egyptians than to die in the wilderness.

Narrator 1: Moses believed that God would save the Israelites. He wanted God's people to believe too. If you were there, you would have heard him say:

Narrator 2: Fear not, stand firm, and see the salvation of the Lord that God will work for you today. He will fight for you, and you have only to be silent.

Narrator 1: Now, hold the streamers at your side. Swing your arms forward and back.

The Lord told Moses to lift up his staff and to stretch out his hand over the sea and divide it. Then Moses was to tell the people of Israel to go through the sea on dry ground. If you were there, you would have seen . . .

Narrator 2: Moses stretch out his hand over the sea. You would have seen the Lord push back the sea and divide the waters. You would have seen the people of Israel walk through the water on dry ground with a wall of water on their right and a wall of water on their left.

Narrator 1: Hold the streamers in front of you. Wave them really fast. Lift them slowly. Together, make a wall of blue to look like the wall of water.

The mighty Egyptians followed the Israelites into the sea. It was frightening, but God was there in the pillar of cloud. If you were there, you would have heard the Lord say to Moses:

Narrator 2: Stretch out your hand over the sea. The water will come back and cover the Egyptians, their chariots, and their horsemen.

Narrator 1: And that is just what happened. Moses stretched out his hand. The waters returned. The Egyptians died.

Lower your streamers and swirl them in circles. Repeat the following words with me. This is how (this is how) the Lord saved Israel (the Lord saved Israel) that day (that day) from the Egyptians (from the Egyptians).

Move your streamers in circles over your head.

God's people saw His great power, and they believed in Him. Then, Moses led the people of Israel in a song to the Lord.

Sing "O Sing to the Lord" (*LSB* 808; CD 2)

Lesson Leaflet Review

To Prepare: Hand out Lesson Leaflet 9.

Discuss the illustration on the leaflet cover by answering the questions provided. Then, open the leaflet to the interior pages. Read through the riddles with the children.

Bible Words

Fear not, stand firm, and see the salvation of the LORD. Exodus 14:13

Say **These were the words of Moses as the Israelites stood in fear of the Egyptians. When the Israelites passed through the Red Sea, they were set free from the Egyptians. When we face our enemies of sin, death, and the devil, we need not fear. We can stand boldly and see the salvation of the Lord.**

The Lord saved the Israelites by parting the waters and allowing them to walk through the Red Sea on dry land. How has the Lord saved us? Allow time for answers. **Yes, Jesus died on the cross for us. Then He rose again to save us from our sins.**

In the waters of Baptism, each of us received the Lord's salvation. These wonderful Bible Words remind us of the power of our Lord to save us against our enemies. Review the benefits of Baptism with "Holy Baptism – Part 2" (CD 22).

Let's do some actions that will help us remember these words.

Have the children repeat the following actions with you:

Say **Fear not,**	*(Spread both hands, palms out, in front of face.)*
stand firm,	*(Bring arms down quickly to side, with a snap.)*
and see the salvation of the LORD.	*(Swing arms forward with palms up, dip knees.)*

Key Point

As God saved the Hebrews through the water of the Red Sea, He saves us through the washing of water in Holy Baptism, conquering Satan, our greatest enemy.

3 We Live (20 minutes)

Growing through God's Word

To Prepare: Use four pieces of construction paper. On each one, write all these words: *sin*, *death*, and the *devil*. Make copies of Activity Page 9B for each child to use along with crayons or markers.

Gather the children together, standing in a huddle. Tell them that they are to pretend that they are in great danger. Tell them that their enemies are on every side of them. On each side of them, use tape to post the signs you have made.

Say **Each of you has three big enemies. They are after you every day. These enemies are outside you as these signs are, coming at you from every direction. These enemies are also inside you, where you can't see them. They want to make you their slaves. Who are these enemies?** Let the children tell. Give concrete examples of temptations (e.g., ignoring parents when asked to put clothes or toys away, not coming when parents call them, throwing a fit when they don't get what they want, complaining about hard work).

Ask the children to sit down and continue.

Say **But you are no longer slaves. You are free. You have been rescued from sin, death, and the devil. To find out how, complete this coloring page.**

Children color in the sections of Activity Page 9B with the water drop to reveal a baptismal font. When they are finished, continue.

Say **God defeated the Egyptians with His mighty power. God defeated our enemies through the power of Jesus' death and resurrection. God saved the Hebrews through the waters of the Red Sea. God gives us His salvation through the waters of Holy Baptism. Each day, Jesus gives us victory over our battles with sinful behavior. Each day, Jesus rescues you from temptation so you can escape from its control.**

Craft Page

To Prepare: Get the CD ready. Hand out Craft Page 9 (Student Book), along with straws (cut in half) and tape.

Cut on the solid line to separate the puppet figures from the Red Sea. Fold up the dotted lines of the section that represents the Red Sea. To make upside-down puppets, cut out the figures and tape a straw half to the *top* of each figure. Allow the children to retell the Bible story using their puppets.

Another option is to make the puppets *before* you tell the story in the "Telling God's Word" section. Let the children use them as props during the storytelling instead of the streamers.

4 Closing (5 minutes)

To Prepare: Use the CD. Gather materials to send home.

Gather the children for the Closing. Follow the same routine each week.

Say **God saved the Israelites through the water of the Red Sea.**

Sing "O Sing to the Lord" (*LSB* 808; CD 2) or "Thank the Lord and Sing His Praise" (*SGL*, p. 41)

Say **Fear not, stand firm, and see the salvation of the Lord** (Exodus 14:13; CD 4)**.**

Challenge Encourage the children to remind others how special Baptism is by making baptismal birthday cards and sending them to people in the congregation or by making a Baptism poster to give to those who will be baptized next in your congregation.

Pray **Dear God, through the power of Jesus' death and resurrection, You have rescued me from all my enemies. Take away my fears, and continue to guide me. In Jesus' name I pray. Amen.**

As the children leave,

Say **God saved you through the waters of Baptism.**

Reflect Do you feel as if there's not enough time for retelling stories? From week to week, save storytelling figures or craft projects in large plastic bags. As children arrive each week, they can retell the stories from previous weeks by using these materials.

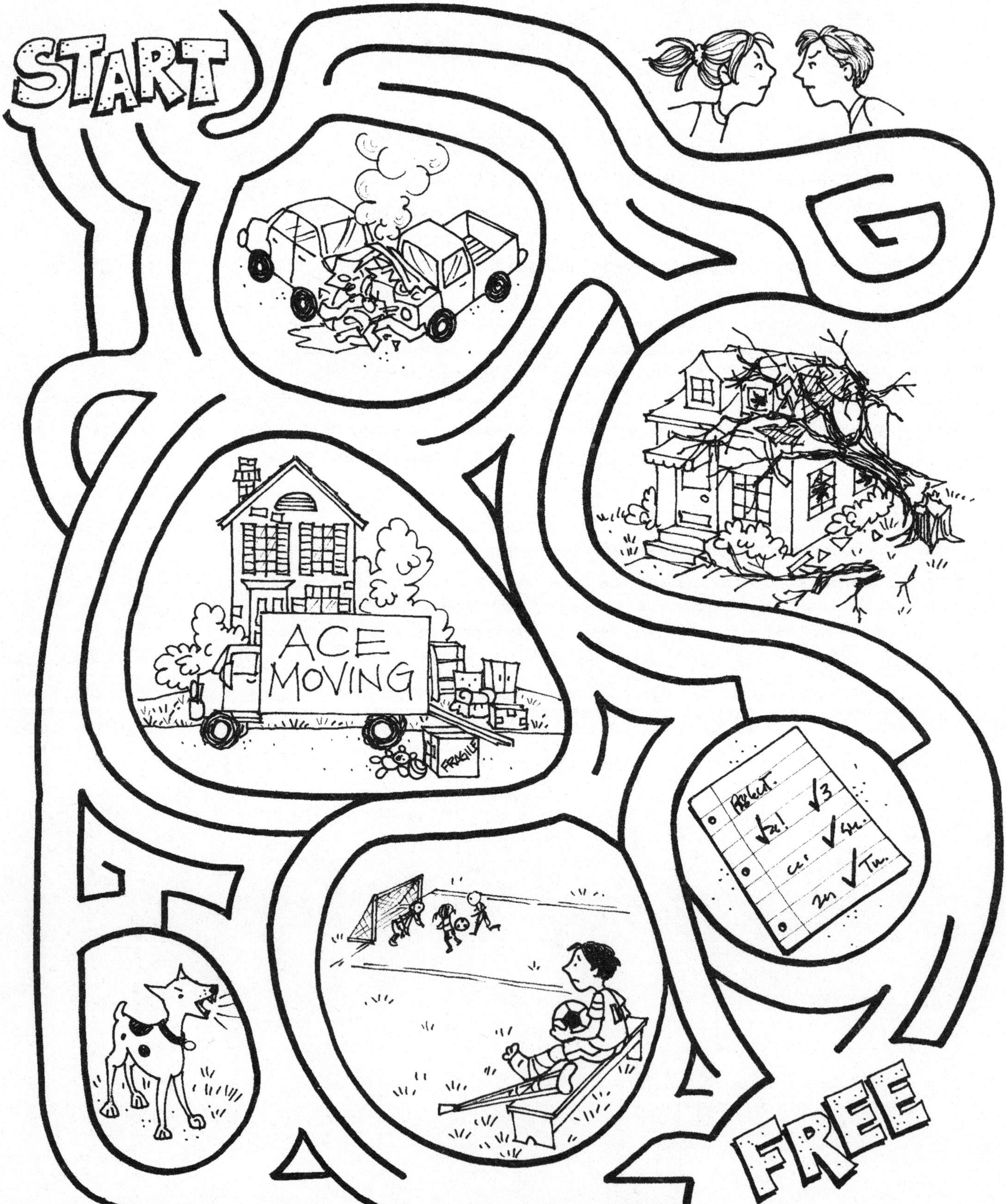
START
ACE
MOVING
FRAGILE
FREE

God s💧ved me through the w💧ter of Holy B💧ptism.

Print the letter *a* in each water drop above. In the picture below, color in each shape where you see a water drop.

Lesson 10

Preparing the Lesson

Date of Use

God Provides Manna, Water, and Quail

Exodus 16–17

Key Point

In Christ, God feeds us with the manna of His Word and the water of His forgiveness, satisfying our eternal hunger and quenching our spiritual thirst.

Law/**Gospel**

My attempts to satisfy myself with all good things cannot fill the void that sin creates in my life. **Christ—by His suffering, death, and resurrection—fills me to overflowing with His life-giving grace and mercy.**

Context

Escaping the clutches of drowned Pharaoh, the Israelites find themselves wandering in the desert without food and water. Humankind, in sinful unbelief, soon begins to grumble about the lack of amenities. Yet, God provides for His people. God "commanded the skies above and opened the doors of heaven, and He rained down on them manna to eat and gave them the grain of heaven" (Psalm 78:23–24). Moreover, God Himself stands before Moses on the rock. As Moses strikes, water gushes forth to quench Israel's thirst.

Commentary

Any number of life's maladies can overwhelm us and leave us hanging out to dry in our deserts of doubt. A job loss or a serious illness can leave us fretting over the basic things of this world, even food and drink.

The Israelites worry too, because they hunger. Sand seemingly scattered everywhere disheartens this group of depressed desert drifters. A Promised Land flowing with milk and honey seems worlds away to ravenous stomachs and dry, chapped lips. This anxious distrust in the Father festers into sinful unbelief.

"Which one of you, if his son asks him for bread, will give him a stone?" (Matthew 7:9). If we, who are evil, know how to give good gifts to our children, how much more will our Father in heaven give good gifts! God always acts against our unbelief. He loves us enough to provide for us. Thus, God rains bread from heaven for His people and creates water from a rock simply by the striking of a staff.

Likewise, our Father gives us the true bread from heaven, Jesus Christ. God provides us His Son so that we "shall not live by bread alone, but by every word that comes from the mouth of God" (Matthew 4:4). In His Word, we partake of the same spiritual rock from which the Israelites drank, for "the Rock was Christ" (1 Corinthians 10:4).

Regardless of the extent of our desert surroundings, we have no worries because God fills us with Christ through His Word! On account of the Lord's atoning sacrifice, His Word speaks absolution. In His Word, forgiveness rains down as manna. Forgiveness pours forth as soothing waters from our Rock's stricken side. This water, infused with grace, quenches our thirsting throats and reinvigorates worry-worn souls. Satiated by the Word, let us with carefree hearts "make a joyful noise to the rock of our salvation!" (Psalm 95:1).

To hear an in-depth discussion of this Bible account, visit cph.org/podcast and listen to our Seeds of Faith podcast each week.

Lesson 10

God Provides Manna, Water, and Quail Exodus 16–17

Connections

Bible Words
Then you shall know that I am the LORD your God. Exodus 16:12

Faith Word
satisfy

Hymn
O Sing to the Lord (*LSB* 808; CD 2)

Catechism
First Commandment

1 Opening (10 minutes)

Introducing Concepts

To Prepare: Post the attendance chart, and set out the offering basket and stickers (Student Pack). Have magazines, scissors, and the box ready. If you have enough devices for small groups of children to share, you may want to have them search the Web for pictures of blessings and "pin" the images to a digital classroom folder instead. Make sure the church has a child-safe filter for Internet searching, or bookmark specific sites they can use.

Greet your students as they arrive. Introduce yourself to any new students, and make sure that they are introduced to the other children. Direct the students to place their offerings in the basket and post their attendance. Then, gather them in a circle.

Say **When we gather, we often thank God for His blessings. Let's look through these magazines and find pictures of things for which we are thankful.**

Children cut out as many pictures as time permits. Some children may have difficulty cutting out pictures. To help, cut out a few pictures before class, and ask if any children would like to use them. Or have children work together, cutting out pictures that may interest another person.

Allow the children to tell about some of the pictures they've cut out. Place the pictures the children have cut out inside the box.

MATERIALS NEEDED

1 Opening	2 God Speaks	3 We Live	4 Closing
Teacher Tools Attendance chart CD **Student Pack** Stickers **Other Supplies** Offering basket Resource Page 1 (TG) Magazines Box Songbook	**Teacher Tools** Poster E Glue stick CD **Student Pack** Lesson Leaflet 10 Stickers **Other Supplies** Lily the puppet Resource Page 2 (TG) Activity Page 10A (TG) Activity Page 10B (TG) Blanket	**Teacher Tools** CD **Student Pack** Craft Page 10 **Other Supplies** Small box Magazine cutouts Activity Page 10A (TG)	**Teacher Tools** CD **Other Supplies** Songbook

Say **God gives us His blessings in many ways. Today, we will hear about an unusual way God gave His blessings.**

Rituals and Routines

To Prepare: If your children gather with others for the Opening, begin teaching with part 2. If you prefer to develop your own opening, a suggested outline follows. For an extended opening, use Resource Page 1 (TG).

Gathering Song: "Thank You, Loving Father" (*SGL*, p. 39; CD 17)

Invocation: **In the name of the Father and of the Son and of the Holy Spirit. Amen.**

Offering

The Commandments: Review the First Commandment (CD 19)

Prayers

Celebrations: Birthdays and Baptism birthdays

2 God Speaks (20 minutes)

Introducing God's Word

To Prepare: Set out a restickable glue stick (available from cph.org), the Faith Words Poster (Poster E), and the Faith Words cards (Resource Page 2) found in the back of the Teacher Guide. This week, cut out the word *satisfy* from the cards. Take out Lily or another puppet.

Lily enters slowly, holding her tummy.

Teacher: Lily, why are you walking so slowly?

Lily: I'm so full! Grandpa made his super yummy pancakes with blueberries for breakfast. I didn't even know we had blueberries in the house. I was surprised!

Teacher: A full tummy feels good. If you were hungry when you woke up, you aren't hungry anymore. You are satisfied.

Lily: Satisfied? Satisfied? What does that mean?

Teacher: Well, it doesn't mean full of pancakes. It means that you are content. Our Faith Word today will help me explain.

Show the Faith Words Poster (Poster E). Ask one of the children to use the glue stick to add the word *satisfy* to the poster.

Teacher: This week's Faith Word is *satisfy*. To satisfy means to give someone something he or she needs or wants. Your grandpa made pancakes this morning to give you food. You need food. Now, you are content. You don't need anything else. You are happy with what you have and don't feel you need any more. You are satisfied.

Lily: I sure am!

Teacher: In our Bible story today, God satisfies the needs of the Israelite people, and He surprises them too.

Telling God's Word

To Prepare: Set up a simple blanket "tent" somewhere in your room by spreading a blanket over a table or several desk tops. Cut out the twelve Blessing Cards from Activity Page 10A. Color the back of four Blessing Cards blue to represent water. Color the back of four Blessing Cards brown to represent quail. Leave four Blessing Cards uncolored to represent manna. Open your Bible and carry it with you as you lead the children around the classroom. For an added touch, use a device to record the children whining and complaining. (You may even want to use a sound effect app to enhance and exaggerate the sound.) Play the recording during the appropriate times in the story.

Say **As the Israelite people traveled through the desert on their way to the Promised Land, they camped in tent homes out in the open, in the wilderness.** "Travel" through your room. Stop at the tent and allow the children to sit underneath. Remind the children to keep their own (personal) space.

Living out in the wilderness wasn't the same as living in Egypt. The people didn't have the same foods and routines. Sometimes, they missed all those things. What do you think they did then? They grumbled. They complained to their leaders, Moses and Aaron. They said that in Egypt, they had more food to eat. They wondered why Moses had brought them out into the wilderness if they were only going to die of hunger.

The Lord told Moses to say to the people, "I have heard your grumblings. Tomorrow at sunset, you shall eat meat. In the morning, you will eat bread. Then you shall know that I am the Lord your God." And it happened just as God promised. At twilight, quail covered the camp. What a surprise! What a blessing! Have a child turn over the Blessing Cards that are brown on the back to represent quail.

In the morning, small drops of water called dew lay around the camp. And when the sun dried up the dew, there was a fine, flakelike thing on the ground. Have some children place the white Blessing Cards facedown to represent manna. **The Israelite people had no name for this food that tasted like wafers made with honey. So they called it manna, a word that means "What is it?" Six days they gathered food, but on the Sabbath Day there was no food. To provide for that day, God told the Israelite people to gather twice as much the day before the Sabbath. Then they could rest on the Sabbath. What a surprise! What a blessing!**

So God cared for the people of Israel and provided them with all the food they needed. "Travel" through your room. **But as they traveled through the wilderness, they grumbled again. They said, "Why did you bring us up out of Egypt? To kill us with thirst?"**

God heard their complaints. To provide water, He told Moses to take his staff and strike the rock. When he did, water came out of the rock. What a surprise! What a blessing! Have a child place the blue Blessing Cards facedown to represent water. **So God cared for the people of Israel and provided them with all the water they needed.**

God satisfied every need the Israelites had as they traveled through the desert on their way to the Promised Land.

After telling the story, place the Blessing Cards in the box with the magazine cutouts.

Lesson Leaflet Review

To Prepare: Hand out Lesson Leaflet 10 and the stickers for this lesson.

Discuss the illustration on the leaflet cover by answering the questions provided. Then open the leaflet to the interior pages. Use these pages to review the Bible story. As children retell the story, they place stickers in the rectangles to show what happened each morning (except the Sabbath) and each evening (except the Sabbath), and what happened at a rock.

Bible Words

Then you shall know that I am the Lord your God. Exodus 16:12

To Prepare: Make copies of Activity Page 10B. Provide scissors and glue or a glue stick. Be prepared to play the First Commandment on the CD.

Say **Moses spoke these words to the Israelites as He told them how God was planning to care for them in the desert. God made the people wait on His grace so that they could know about His love. They seemed to have forgotten that God was doing what was best for them.**

Ask **How did the Israelite people show that they were not trusting in God when they were first in the desert?** Allow time for answers. **That's right! The Israelites grumbled and complained about their life in the desert. They had forgotten that the Lord their God was always with them, ready to care for them. Let's do an activity that will help us remember these Bible Words, which tell us that God is always with us too, providing for all our needs.**

Give each child a copy of Activity Page 10B, scissors, and glue. Direct the children to cut out the words and place them in the correct order on the Bible.

While they are working, remind the children of the words of the First Commandment. "You shall have no other gods." *What does this mean?* "We should fear, love and trust in God above all things." Find these words on the CD.

Say **With our own power, we cannot have this kind of love and trust. We think we're doing fine on our own and don't need God. We look to other things besides God to satisfy us and make us happy and content. Those things aren't necessarily bad, but when we look to them first, instead of God, then we are breaking the First Commandment.**

However, by the mercy of God's forgiveness and the power of His love in Jesus Christ, we can love God more than sports, more than movies and shows, more than games—more than anything. Christ obeyed the First Commandment for us, and He took our penalty for not obeying it. By His dying and rising, we are right with God. We can trust God to preserve our lives, to satisfy our needs.

There will be days when we still do not trust God to provide for us. We will grumble and complain. When we sin in this way, God is ready to forgive us and bless us for Jesus' sake. We can ask Him to forgive us, and we know that He will.

Key Point

In Christ, God feeds us with the manna of His Word and the water of His forgiveness, satisfying our eternal hunger and quenching our spiritual thirst.

3 We Live (20 minutes)

Growing through God's Word

To Prepare: Set out Poster H and the Blessings Box filled with the magazine cutouts and Blessing Cards. You will also need a pair of scissors. Place the box behind Poster H. *Note*: Poster H will also be used with the story of the Ten Commandments.

Great Idea!

Say **I'm going to put the Blessings Box behind the picture of this cross. Because we are sinners, we don't deserve anything from God except punishment. We are no different from the grumbling, mumbling Israelite people. We often don't look first to God to satisfy our needs. We don't trust that He knows what's best for us, so we look to other things to get what we want.**

We deserve to die. But God is merciful. Pick up the scissors. **He sent His Son, Jesus, to suffer and die on the cross to take away our sin.** Poke the scissors on one edge of the cross, and carefully cut out only the cross. **Because of Jesus, God doesn't see our sin. Through Jesus, we have blessings in our lives. God blesses us with things that we need and with extra things—things we are happy to have in our lives. You may not have *all* you want or the *exact kind* of thing that you want, but God gives you what you *need*.**

I want you to reach through the cross and pull out a blessing from the Blessing Box. Together, we'll say thank You to God for whatever blessing you find.

Continue holding up the poster. As each child takes a turn pulling out a blessing, have the group thank God together for that item. For example, if someone pulls out a picture of shoes, the group could say, "Thank You, God, for our shoes." When you are finished with the prayers, sing a song or do one more activity with the pictures.

Sing "Thank the Lord and Sing His Praise" (*SGL*, p. 41, CD 16) or "God Is So Good" (*SGL*, p. 62; CD 8).

Option: Use the melody of "God Is So Good" along with the lyrics "He gives me . . ." Fill in the song with words that identify the blessing from the Blessing Box.

Say **Jesus fills us to overflowing with His mercy.** After the prayer, have the children share their picture with a friend, giving it to him or her to keep (or if there are more pictures in the box, reach back through and take another one). **We have all that we need and enough blessings to share with others in need.**

Craft Page

To Prepare: Hand out Craft Page 10 (Student Book) along with scissors and transparent tape. Make copies of the Blessing Cards (Activity Page 10A) for each student.

This week, each child will make a Blessings Basket. Cut along the solid lines. The large rectangle will become the base of the basket. Fold over the tabs along the dotted lines. Tape the tabs to the sides of the basket. Tape the handle (the strip with the Bible Words on it) to the edge of the basket. Children can collect the blessings that they cut out from the magazines and place them in their baskets. Give each child copies of the Blessing Cards from Activity Page 10A to put in their baskets.

Ask **Where could you put your Blessings Basket? How could you use it this week?** Allow the children time to think of an answer. **You could use your Blessings Basket as a centerpiece on your table to remind your family that God satisfies all of our needs with wonderful blessings, which you receive through Jesus Christ, your Savior. We don't need to worry or look to something else to meet our needs. We trust and hope in the Lord our God!**

4 Closing (5 minutes)

To Prepare: Use the CD. Gather materials to send home.

Gather the children for the Closing. Follow the same routine each week.

Say **God satisfied the needs of the Israelite people with manna, quail, and water.**

Sing "He Cares for Me" (*SGL*, p. 57; CD 12) or "Praise and Thanksgiving" (*SGL*, p. 39; CD 15)

Say **Then you shall know that I am the LORD your God** (Exodus 16:12).

Challenge Tell the children about special "bread" or "water" ministries at your congregation or in the community. Encourage the children to participate (donate water bottles to a community without good drinking water, help a parent to bake banana bread to take to new families at church or in the community, and the like).

Pray **Dear God, thank You for the many blessings You give me through the sacrifice of Jesus, my Savior. Amen.**

As the children leave,

Say **God satisfies all your needs.**

Reflect Do the children help one another on projects? Through your words, notice these positive traits in children. Children working together in a classroom setting build a wonderful sense of community.

Blessing Cards

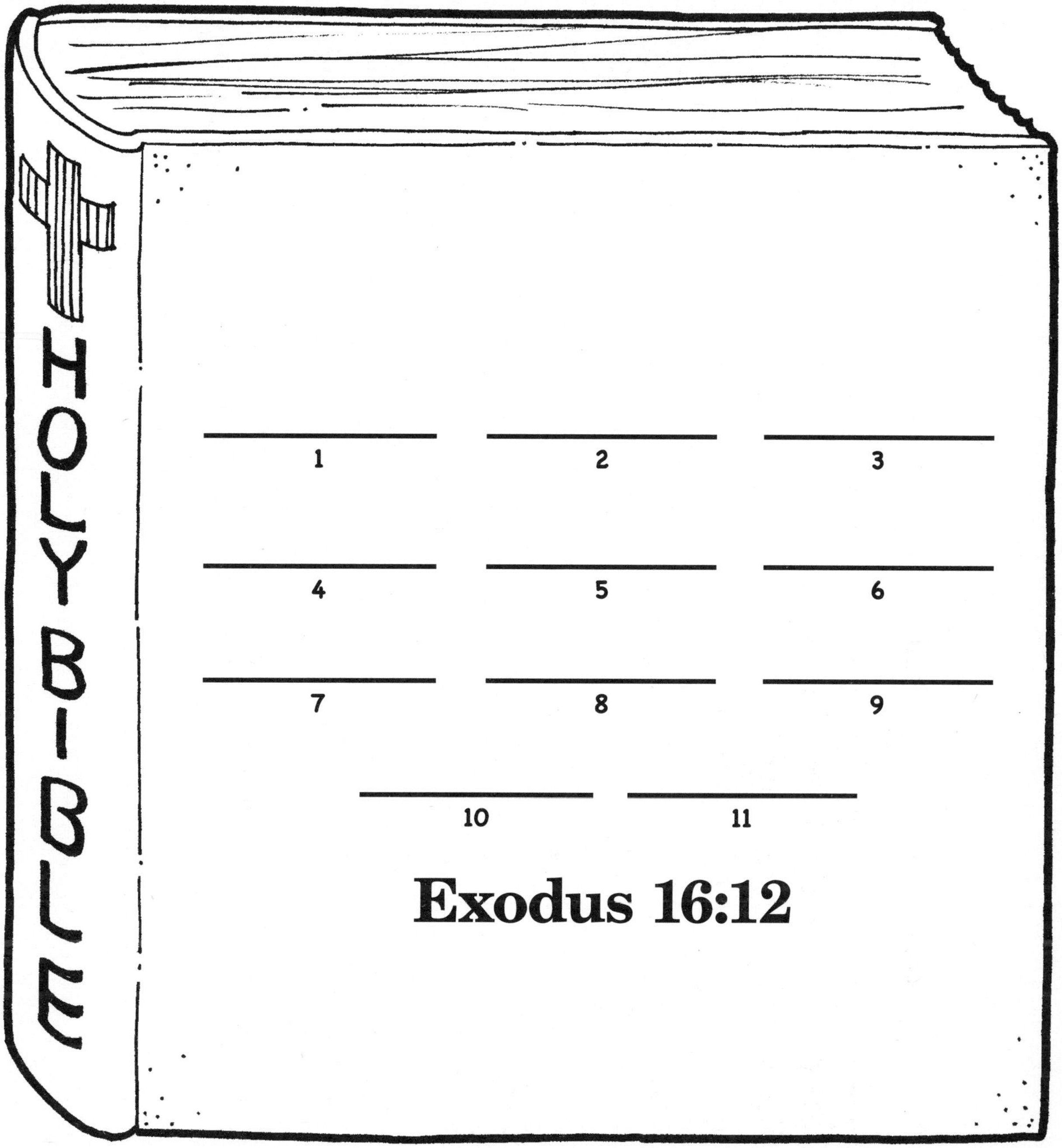

Cut out the words below. Glue them in order so that you can read today's Bible Words from Exodus 16:12.

Then 1	LORD 9	shall 3	God 11	that 5
I 6	know 4	you 2	am 7	your 10
the 8				

Lesson 11

Date of Use

Preparing the Lesson

The Ten Commandments

Exodus 19–20

Key Point

The Law kills, but the Gospel revives. "For the law was given through Moses; grace and truth came through Jesus Christ" (John 1:17).

Law/Gospel

The Ten Commandments define God's Law. **Jesus, through His incarnation and by His suffering and death for my sins, defines God's love and mercy toward me.**

Context

In the burning bush, God answers Moses' question, saying, "When you have brought the people out of Egypt, you shall serve God on this mountain" (Exodus 3:12). God fulfills this promise and delivers the Israelites to the base of Mount Sinai. Here, in the midst of the smoldering smoke that shrouds the summit, God gives Moses the Ten Commandments.

Commentary

After parting the seas for us, showering us with manna from heaven, and bringing forth water from a rock to quench our thirst, the Lord prepares to give us a far superior gift. "Let them . . . be ready for the third day" (Exodus 19:10–11), because the Law is coming.

The great cloud descends first "like the smoke of a kiln" (Exodus 19:18), blocking out the light and obscuring our view. Next, we hear the deafening trumpet of God Himself purifying the air before His holy presence. At the sound, the soldiers lift their spears, ready to carry out the Lord's orders. Should a person's hand or foot touch the mountain, "he shall not live" (Exodus 19:13). Our eardrums nearly burst from the thunderclaps as lightning flashes threateningly all around us. Last, God's condemning voice rains vocal death on us in the proclamation of the Ten Commandments. Fear chills the very marrow of our shaking souls as we realize that we can never keep such holy commands.

Through the haze of our singed, stinging, and tear-filled eyes, we see an unassuming figure step forward through the cowering crowd. His broken and bruised back, anointed by the bloodied whip, bears our Law-demanded cross. As He steps on that mountain in our stead, He willingly acquires our death sentence. The soldiers carry out God's command, crucifying Christ. This "man of sorrows" (Isaiah 53:3) pours out His soul to death and is numbered with the transgressors (Isaiah 53:12). The mountains tremble, a cloud of darkness descends, and a soldier spears the One who came not "to abolish the Law or the Prophets" but "to fulfill them" (Matthew 5:17).

Indeed, let us be ready for the third day. The Law kills, but the Gospel revives. When the final earthquakes of the Law reverberate and die on that third day, a tomb sits empty. At this tomb, His angel soothes our ears with His peace-packed proclamation: "Do not be afraid. . . . He is not here, for He has risen, as He said" (Matthew 28:5–6).

While "the law was given through Moses, grace and truth came through Jesus Christ" (John 1:17). Tears of fear melt into joy. May we always live in Christ, through whom "everyone who believes is freed from everything from which you could not be freed by the law of Moses" (Acts 13:38–39).

To hear an in-depth discussion of this Bible account, visit cph.org/podcast and listen to our Seeds of Faith podcast each week.

Lesson 11

The Ten Commandments

Exodus 19–20

Connections

Bible Words
The law was given through Moses; grace and truth came through Jesus Christ. John 1:17

Faith Word
Law

Hymn
O Sing to the Lord (*LSB* 808; CD 2)

Catechism
The Ten Commandments

1 Opening (10 minutes)

Introducing Concepts

To Prepare: Post the attendance chart, provide stickers (attendance and those for Introducing Concepts), and set out the offering basket. Have a half sheet of paper (black, if possible) for each child.

Greet your students as they arrive. Introduce yourself to any new students, and make sure that they are introduced to the other children. Direct the students to place their offerings in the basket and post their attendance. Then, gather them in a circle. Give a half sheet of black craft paper and the three colored stickers for this activity to each child. An alternative activity would be to play an online "stoplight" or "stop and go" children's game using a large screen, so all the children can play at the same time. Preview before class.

Say **Let's make a stoplight out of this paper and these stickers. Does anyone know the order of the colors? Which color is on top?** (Red) **Which color is in the middle?** (Yellow) **Which color is on the bottom?** (Green) Give children time to place the stickers on the sheet in the correct positions. **Can anyone explain how stoplights are used?** Allow time for the children to answer.

Say **There is a law in our country that says we must stop when we see a red stoplight. Why is that a good thing? Why is it a bad thing if someone doesn't stop?** Give the children time to answer.

Ask **Can anyone think of any other laws in our country or city? Today, we'll hear about a set of rules that God gave His people and a way they could be sure to keep them.**

MATERIALS NEEDED

1 Opening	2 God Speaks	3 We Live	4 Closing
Teacher Tools Attendance chart CD **Student Pack** Stickers **Other Supplies** Offering basket Resource Page 1 (TG) Songbook Black paper	**Teacher Tools** CD Poster E Glue stick **Student Pack** Lesson Leaflet 11 Stickers **Other Supplies** Resource Page 2 (TG) Activity Page 11A (TG) Stoplights Activity Page 11B (TG)	**Teacher Tools** Poster H CD **Student Pack** Craft Page 11 Stickers **Other Supplies** Green paper or plastic cups Small box Green construction paper (optional)	**Teacher Tools** CD **Other Supplies** Songbook

Rituals and Routines

To Prepare: If your children gather with others for the Opening, begin teaching with part 2. If you prefer to develop your own opening, a suggested outline follows. For an extended opening, use Resource Page 1 (TG).

Gathering Song: "There Is a Name I Love to Hear" (*SGL*, p. 50)

Invocation: **In the name of the Father and of the Son and of the Holy Spirit. Amen.**

Offering

The Commandments: Review the First Commandment (CD 19)

Prayers

Celebrations: Birthdays and Baptism birthdays

2 God Speaks (20 minutes)

Introducing God's Word

To Prepare: Set out a copy of Activity Page 11A, scissors, a restickable glue stick (available from cph.org), the Faith Words Poster (Poster E), and the Faith Words cards (Resource Page 2) found in the back of the Teacher Guide. This week, cut out the word *Law* from the cards.

Show the Faith Words Poster (Poster E), and introduce today's Faith Word.

Say **This week's Faith Word is *Law.*** Ask one of the children to use the glue stick to add the word *Law* on the Faith Words Poster. **In today's Bible story, God gives the Israelite people laws. Many of the laws are like the stoplight and remind hearers to stop doing something. Others are like the go signal and tell hearers what to do.**

Let's use these strips to help us find out more about how God gave the Ten Commandments and what they are. Distribute the strips to the children. Give each child at least one (or more than one, depending on the size of your classroom). **As we listen to today's Bible story, we will place the commandments in order.**

Read through each commandment together.

Telling God's Word

To Prepare: Make copies of the commandment strips from Activity Page 11A. Today's Bible story is on the CD.

Before you begin the CD, open a Bible and tell the children that the story they will hear comes from the Book of Exodus in the Bible.

Say **When you hear the commandment that is on your paper, lay the slip of paper in front of the group.** Set it down or post it where all can see.

Narrator: As the Israelite people camped beneath Mount Sinai (SIGH nih eye) in the desert, God called to Moses from the mountain. He said,

God: Tell the people of Israel this news. You have seen what I did to the Egyptians and how I brought you to Myself. Now if you will obey Me and keep My covenant, you shall be My treasured possession among all peoples.

Narrator: So Moses told all of the people the words that the Lord had told him. The Israelite people were happy. They wanted to be God's people. When God heard this news, He told Moses,

God: Behold, I am coming to you in a thick cloud, so that the people may hear when I speak with you. I want them to believe in Me forever.

Narrator: So one morning soon after that, the people saw lightning. They saw the mountain smoking. They heard thunder and a loud trumpet blast. They trembled in fear as Moses brought them out of the camp to meet God. They did not want to go into the thick cloud. So Moses went into the thick cloud. God spoke all the words of the Ten Commandments to Moses from a cloud on a mountain called Mount Sinai. He said,

God: I am the Lord your God, who brought you out of the land of Egypt, out of the house of slavery.
You shall have no other gods.
You shall not misuse the name of the LORD your God.
Remember the Sabbath (SAB bahth) day by keeping it holy.
Honor your father and your mother.
You shall not murder.
You shall not commit adultery.
You shall not steal.
You shall not give false testimony against your neighbor.
You shall not covet your neighbor's house.
You shall not covet your neighbor's wife, or his manservant or maidservant, his ox or donkey, or anything that belongs to your neighbor.

Narrator: God wanted His treasured possessions to learn the Ten Commandments and to know them well. He wanted to be their only God, number one in their lives.

When the CD is finished, review the Commandments again, using Luther's Small Catechism. As you do, ask the children to hold up their stoplights. When a commandment speaks about something we *should* do, children point to the green section. If a commandment speaks about something we *should not* do, children point to the red section. As each commandment is read, explain any vocabulary the children do not understand.

Lesson Leaflet Review

To Prepare: Hand out Lesson Leaflet 11 and stickers for the Lesson Leaflet Review.

Discuss the questions on the leaflet cover. Then open the leaflet to the interior pages to review the Bible story. Children use the numbered stickers to put the commandments in order. To help review the order, use the strips from Activity Page 11A.

Bible Words

The law was given through Moses; grace and truth came through Jesus Christ. John 1:17

To Prepare: Have copies of Activity Page 11B and pencils ready.

Write the Bible Words on the board or on a large piece of paper. Above the words, draw an arching arrow from the word *law* to the word *Moses.* Draw an arrow arching from the words *grace* and *truth* to the words *Jesus Christ.* Refer to the drawing as you speak.

Say **God gave His Law, the Ten Commandments, to Moses so that Moses could tell it to the people. Sometimes we use a drawing of two stone tablets to represent God's Law.** Draw two stone tablets by (below) the word *law.* **We are God's people too. His Law is for us. God demands that we keep His Ten Commandments, every "you shall" and every "you shall not."**

Can we keep God's Law? Some students may believe that they can. Clarify this point. **No, we cannot keep God's Law perfectly. We say bad words, we are mean to others, we lie, we cheat, and we steal.**

Whom did God send to keep the Law for us? Allow time for answers. **Yes, God sent Jesus to be our Savior. Jesus kept the Law—all of these Commandments—perfectly.** Draw a cross by (below) the words *Jesus Christ.* **Jesus never said bad words. He never lied or cheated on a test or took things that weren't His. God sent Jesus to do this for us because we couldn't keep the Law ourselves. God sent Jesus to suffer and die on the cross to pay the price we should have paid for breaking the Law. Jesus' death paid for our sins. Through Jesus, we receive two things. What are they?** (Grace and truth) Underline the words *grace* and *truth.*

Review the cues on the Lesson Leaflet. Ask the children to repeat the Bible Words. Then hand out Activity Page 11B (TG). Children follow the directions on the page to complete the Bible Words.

Sing "O Sing to the Lord" (*LSB* 808; CD 2). Rejoice that God is the Lord and loves us enough to give us rules for our good. There is no one like God. Rejoice that God loves us enough to send Jesus to be our Lord and Savior!

Key Point

The Law kills, but the Gospel revives. "The law was given through Moses; grace and truth came through Jesus Christ" (John 1:17).

3 We Live (20 minutes)

Growing through God's Word

To Prepare: Set out Poster H with the top of the cross cut out. (Poke the scissors on one edge of the cross and carefully cut out only the cross.) Set out the box, the Ten Commandment strips, strips of paper, and the stickers for this section.

Place the small box behind Poster H.

Say **The commandment strips go in this box for safekeeping. They are God's Law for us. If we obey them, God will know that we love Him. God is perfect, and He expects us to be perfect too. Following God's rules will make us right with God. But, you have a problem with being perfect. So do I.**

Sometimes, we make other things more important than God. We do not always honor our parents. At times, we are jealous of our friends, brothers, or sisters. It is impossible for us to keep the Law perfectly. We cannot be right with God because we cannot do everything He commands us to do in His Law.

Whom did God send to keep His Law perfectly for us? Yes, Jesus came to be our Savior. He kept God's Law perfectly and died on the cross to save us from our sin. His death paid the price of our sin.

To illustrate this, ask each child to put his or her name on a slip of paper and mark the paper with the sticker from the Student Pack that says *Guilty*. Then have each student ceremonially, one at a time, put his or her paper through the cut-out cross and into the box. Through the cross opening, hand that child the sticker that says *Forgiven Child of God*. The children can wear their stickers.

Say **God loved us so much that He gave Jesus to die for us, so that we could be made right with God and be saved. We are God's treasured possessions. We are His forgiven children. Each morning, we can be reassured of His love and care. Each morning, we are a new person; our sins are gone! Through Jesus, we see God's love and mercy.**

Craft Page

To Prepare: Hand out Craft Page 11 (Student Book). Have the CD, scissors, green paper or plastic cups, and glue sticks or tape ready. If you can't find green cups, roll a half sheet of green construction paper into a cylinder and tape so it is sturdy and will stand upright. Or use a different colored cup.

Cut out the commandment tablets and the cross along the outer edges. Tape or staple the cross to the side of an upside-down paper cup. Fold the tablets on the middle line so the Bible Words show on the top and the commandments are on the inside. Use the glue stick or tape to attach the tablets to the opposite side of the "hill" (paper cup and cross).

Ask **How does this craft remind you of today's Bible Words? God gave the Law to Moses on Mount Sinai. Jesus kept God's Law perfectly. Then He died for our sins on the hill at Calvary. And through faith in our Savior Jesus, we receive God's grace and truth.**

4 Closing (5 minutes)

To Prepare: Use the CD. Gather materials to send home.

Gather the children for the Closing. Follow the same routine each week.

Say **In love, God gave His Law to the Israelite people. In love, God gave His Son to save sinners.**

Sing "Jesus Loves Me, This I Know" (*SGL*, p. 51) or "God Loved the World So That He Gave" (*LSB* 571; CD 9)

Say **The law was given through Moses; grace and truth came through Jesus Christ** (John 1:17)**.**

Challenge Encourage the children to forgive someone this week. If their friend or a family member takes something of theirs, calls them a name, uses a swear word, or breaks any of the other Commandments, they can remember that no one is perfect except Jesus, who kept the Law for us and took the punishment we deserved.

Faith in Action!

Pray **Dear God, thank You for sending Jesus to keep the Law for me so that I can be Your child forever. Amen.**

As the children leave,

Say **Jesus kept God's Law for you! You are His treasured possessions.**

Reflect If children become confused during the lesson, do you help them work it out? It's important to spend time talking through whatever is not making sense, so that better learning can occur. And although we talked about ten commandments today, remember that in your classroom, just a few simple rules clearly explained, often reviewed, and consistently applied can make a big difference in the behavior of your students.

You shall have no other gods.
You shall not misuse the name of the Lord your God.
Remember the Sabbath day, to keep it holy.
Honor your father and your mother.
You shall not murder.
You shall not commit adultery.
You shall not steal.
You shall not give false testimony against your neighbor.
You shall not covet your neighbor's house.
You shall not covet your neighbor's wife, or his manservant or maidservant, his ox or donkey, or anything that belongs to your neighbor.

Bible Words Puzzle

1. Add the letter a where you see a blank line.
2. Add the letter t in each triangle.
3. Add the letter g in each oval.
4. Draw a picture in each square.

▽he l__w w__s

◯iven ▽hrou◯h

□ ; ◯r__ce __nd

Draw Moses.

▽ru▽h c__me

▽hrou◯h

□ . John 1:17 □

Draw Jesus Christ.

Draw a Bible.

Lesson 12

Preparing the Lesson

Date of Use

Worship in the Tabernacle

Exodus 40

Key Point

In the tabernacle, God dwelled with His people, cleansing them and making them holy through the blood of sacrifices. In Christ, God now dwells among us, cleansing us and making us holy through Jesus' blood, shed for us on the cross.

Law/**Gospel**

My sin makes me unholy and separates me from God; I am unworthy to stand in His presence. **God cleanses me, makes me holy, and dwells in me through the once-for-all sacrifice of Christ.**

Context

The Israelites are camped at Sinai, almost a year after their exodus from Egypt. The Ten Commandments have been received . . . and almost immediately shattered when the golden calf is constructed. But God has provided a means of atonement for the people: the altar and blood of sacrifice.

The Lord has shown Moses a heavenly tabernacle after which he is to model the earthly tabernacle. Earth reflects heaven. Indeed, heaven is present on earth as the heavenly Lord takes up residence within the tabernacle. Afterward, as recorded in Leviticus, the Lord will institute the various sacrifices by which He will maintain fellowship with His nation.

Commentary

Eden was a sanctuary of sorts, where humans lived and worked in perfect communion with God. But in the post-Eden world, where death and sin strangled creation, where were humans to turn? Where was the "Eden" where they could be made right with God? The Lord made a new garden. The tabernacle became this new Eden for all fallen Adams and Eves. Here, they could return to the Lord and be purified and made holy through the bloody sacrifices instituted by God for their sake. The place even had the look of a garden, with various flora and fauna woven into the very fabric of the tent. Everything about the sanctuary visually proclaimed, "Welcome home, sons of Adam and daughters of Eve! Welcome back to Eden!"

As Eden opened on the east (Genesis 3:24), so did the tabernacle. There, Israelites reentered God's holy place via the altar, and *only* via the altar. There, the blood of bulls, goats, sheep, and doves was poured out. This blood was not simple blood, but blood ordained by God through His Word. God did not need it; sinners did. The sacrifices were for their benefit. By it, they were cleaned, renewed, and made holy.

God's dwelling within the tabernacle also foreshadowed a future, more intimate dwelling of God among people. For the Word became flesh and dwelt (literally, "tabernacled") among us (John 1:14). The Son made our flesh His own; the Creator assumed the stuff of His own creation. His body is our tabernacle, holy and pure.

Baptized into His pure and holy body, we are pure and holy also. We enter where no Old Testament high priest ever could: into the body of God Himself. He cleanses and sanctifies us. Through His once-for-all sacrifice, we are welcomed back into a new Eden: the Church.

Exodus 40 stresses that Moses made everything exactly as God instructed him. Nothing was done willy-nilly; for just as everything in creation had its right place, so in this place of new creation, everything had its right place. For here, God re-created fallen sinners, refashioned them in His image, and restored them to fellowship with Him. In doing all this, He gave an ongoing preview of what He would do in His Son, who is our Tabernacle, our Priest, our Sacrifice, and our Holiness.

To hear an in-depth discussion of this Bible account, visit cph.org/podcast and listen to our Seeds of Faith podcast each week.

Lesson 12

Worship in the Tabernacle

Exodus 40

Connections

Bible Words

Oh give thanks to the LORD, for He is good. Psalm 107:1 (CD 6)

Faith Word

tabernacle

Hymn

O Sing to the Lord (*LSB* 808; CD 2)

Catechism

Holy Baptism

1 Opening (10 minutes)

Introducing Concepts

To Prepare: Post the attendance chart. Set out the stickers (Student Pack) and an offering basket. Make individual copies of Activity Page 12 (TG) at the end of this lesson, and provide pencils or crayons.

Greet your students as they arrive. Introduce yourself to any new students, and make sure that they are introduced to the other children. Direct the students to place their offerings in the basket and post their attendance. Then, gather them in a circle.

In this week's lesson, we learn that God desires to dwell, or live, in the midst of His people. To begin, complete Activity Page 12. Talk about the desire we have to dwell with those we love. Show the maze.

Building Relationships!

Say **Think about someone you like to visit. Pretend you are that person at the bottom of this page and want to get to his or her house. Draw a path through the maze to get to the house. Then write a sentence or draw a picture to tell why you like to be with your friend.**

As the children finish, have them gather together and share their responses. This is a good opportunity for them to get to know each other better or maybe even to be affirmed in their own friendships, if they chose the house of a friend in class. Be alert and sensitive to any children who may have tension at their own home.

MATERIALS NEEDED

1 Opening	2 God Speaks	3 We Live	4 Closing
Teacher Tools Attendance chart **Student Pack** Stickers **Other Supplies** Activity Page 12 (TG) Resource Page 1 (TG; optional)	**Teacher Tools** Poster E Glue stick Background A, Storytelling Figures CD **Student Pack** Lesson Leaflet 12 Stickers (optional) **Other Supplies** Resource Page 2 (TG)	**Student Pack** Craft Page 12 **Other Supplies** Labels	**Teacher Tools** CD **Student Pack** Stickers CD Bible Words (Student Book) **Other Supplies** Activity Page 12 (TG)

Say **What is special about the person living there?** Let the children share. **It's fun to visit friends or family. We look forward to visiting them and sharing special times with them at their home. In today's Bible lesson, we hear about someone who loves to visit us.**

The children will add a sticker to Activity Page 12 in today's closing activity. Make sure the children put their names on their paper; set them aside for later use.

Rituals and Routines

To Prepare: If your children gather with others for the Opening, begin teaching with part 2. If you prefer to develop your own opening, a suggested outline follows. For an extended opening, use Resource Page 1 (TG).

Gathering Song: "We Are in God's House Today" (*SGL*, p. 84)

Invocation: **In the name of the Father and of the Son and of the Holy Spirit. Amen.**

Offering

The Commandments: Review the First Commandment (CD 19)

Prayers

Celebrations: Birthdays and Baptism birthdays

2 God Speaks (20 minutes)

Introducing God's Word

To Prepare: Set out a restickable glue stick (available from cph.org), the Faith Words Poster (Poster E), and the Faith Words cards (Resource Page 2) found in the back of the Teacher Guide. This week, cut out the word *tabernacle* from the cards.

Say **This week's Faith Word is *tabernacle.*** Ask one of the children to use the glue stick to add the word on the poster. **In our Bible story from the Book of Exodus, God tells Moses how to build a special tent so that He could dwell, or be, with His people.** Draw a tent on the board. **Let's find out how that happened. And keep in mind that this was God's house, what today we also call His *sanctuary*. Today, a sanctuary is the part of the church building that has the altar in it; it's where God comes to us in Word and Sacrament.**

Telling God's Word

To Prepare: Set out Table Tent Background A and Storytelling Figures 12-1 through 12-8. With the glue stick, add the figures to the background where indicated during the storytelling. As an alternate background, create a diagram on a whiteboard. See Lesson Leaflet 12 for an example. To enhance the description of the tabernacle, you may want to show images of it found online.

Invite the children to join in the refrain.

Say **Help tell the Bible story. When I point to you, repeat what I say and do.** Point to children and say,

I want to dwell with you. (*Point upward and then wrap arms in front of body.*)

Active Learning Idea!

The background shows the wilderness where the tabernacle was moved from place to place. Tell the children you will show them the furnishings that were used inside the tabernacle. They can pretend the pieces are standing just outside the curtain of the tabernacle, ready to be placed inside.

Let's begin. Place Moses (12-1) next to the cloud (12-8). **Moses went to the top of Mount Sinai. There, God spoke to him. Through Moses, God gave His people the Ten Commandments. God said, "I am your God, and you are My children."** Point to the children and say, **"I want to dwell with you."** (*Point upward and then wrap arms in front of body.*) **God also gave Moses this command: "Build Me a home—a tabernacle, a tent in the middle of My people."** Point to the children and say, **"I want to dwell with you."** (*Point upward and then wrap arms in front of body.*) Remove the cloud (12-8).

So Moses told the people this wonderful news. To build this tabernacle, the people brought gifts. They made beautiful furnishings, using wood, gold, animal hides, and linen—a special cloth that was woven and dyed.

Once everything was built, Moses instructed the people to set up the tabernacle following God's direction. Put the ark (12-2) to the left. **A beautiful golden box, the ark of the covenant, was placed inside a special room. Inside the box were the stones on which God had written the Ten Commandments. On the top of the box, two angels bowed down, looking at a special place called the Mercy Seat. Outside the curtain that separated this room from the next was a beautiful golden lampstand.** Place lampstand (12-3) to the right of the ark, leaving some room. **Each day, morning and evening, the priests trimmed the lamp wicks and made sure there was plenty of oil in the lamps. The light reminded the priests of what God had told Moses.** Point to the children and say, **"I want to dwell with you."** (*Point upward and then wrap arms in front of body.*)

In the Holy Place of the tent of meeting was a table for some bread called the bread of the Presence. Place the table with bread (12- 4) next to lampstand. **On this table, the priests placed twelve loaves of flat bread that looked something like pita bread. When the priests saw the bread or ate the bread, they were reminded of how God took care of them and all His children.**

Inside this Holy Place, there was also a golden altar of incense on which they burned a mixture of sweet-smelling ingredients—God's special recipe. Add the golden altar of incense (12-5). **The burning incense was a reminder that the prayers of God's people were rising toward heaven. God's people knew He would hear their prayers. Remember what He said.** Point to the children and say, **"I want to dwell with you."** (*Point upward and then wrap arms in front of body.*)

Outside those two rooms was a large area, or courtyard. Instead of walls made of wood, the courtyard of the tabernacle was made of fabric. Near the door into the courtyard was a large container of water. The priests used this water for washing. Place basin (12-6) to the right of the bread table, leaving some space. **God told Moses to add something, a special altar, to this courtyard. He said, "At the entrance to the tabernacle, offer Me sacrifices of grain and burnt offerings."** Place bronze altar (12-7) to the far right.

When everything was in place, something amazing happened—the glory of the Lord filled the tabernacle. Place the cloud (12-8) as high as possible. **God's cloud could be seen throughout the area where God's people camped.**

During all their travels, the cloud of the Lord was with His children. The tabernacle was in the center of their tents. When they saw the cloud above the tabernacle, they remembered what God had told Moses. Point to the children and say, **"I want to dwell with you."** (*Point upward and then wrap arms in front of body.*)

To review the lesson, distribute the storytelling figures to the children. Ask them to explain the significance of the tabernacle's furnishings, focusing on God's desire to dwell with His people.

Lesson Leaflet Review

To Prepare: Hand out Lesson Leaflet 12 (Student Book) and a pencil to each child.

Discuss the illustration on the leaflet cover. Then open the leaflet to the interior pages. Read the directions together. The children help the priests set up the tabernacle by drawing a line from the numbered furnishing to its location. In addition, follow the arrows around the courtyard to find the letters. Write the letters on the lines to fill in the blanks. Answer: God dwells with (child fills in his or her name).

Bible Words

Oh give thanks to the Lord, for He is good. Psalm 107:1 (CD 6)

To Prepare: Use the CD to help teach the Bible Words.

Say **In the tabernacle, God dwelled with His people. Because the people were sinful, they offered sacrifices to God, asking Him to forgive their sins and make them holy. They were thankful for God's forgiveness, guidance, and care. They might have said, "Oh give thanks to the Lord, for He is good."**

In His Word, God tells us that He sent His Son to dwell with us. Who is God's Son? (Jesus) **Yes, Jesus came to dwell with us. Because we are sinful, we needed Jesus to be the sacrifice for our sin and to make us holy. In our Baptism, God's Spirit came to dwell within us, forgiving our sins and making us holy. For all this, we say, "Oh give thanks to the Lord, for He is good."**

Play the Bible Words on the CD. You may also want to play "Holy Baptism – Part 2" (CD 22).

3 We Live (20 minutes)

Key Point

In the tabernacle, God dwelled with His people, cleansing them and making them holy through the blood of sacrifices. In Christ, God now dwells among us, cleansing us and making us holy through Jesus' blood, shed for us on the cross.

Growing through God's Word

To Prepare: Write the following words on separate labels, or use a set from Craft Page 12. The words are *Adam, Eve, Jesus, cross, tabernacle, church, Baptism, water, bread, wine, music, praise, hands, pray, glory, cloud.*

Say **Sin makes us unholy. It separates us from God.** Spread your hands far apart. **But God sees what Jesus did for us on the cross.** Make the sign of the cross. **He died for our sins and makes us holy. His Spirit dwells in us.**

Today, we're going to play a game. We'll talk about how Jesus makes us holy and that we are no longer separated from God. Move your hands back together. **He dwells with us.**

Here is how we'll play the game. I will give each person a word. You then find a person with a word that goes with your word. Once you've found that person and word, stand together. Be prepared to tell how your words go together.

At the end of the activity, let the children explain how their words belong together. If needed, use the following explanations to help them.

Say ***Adam* and *Eve* were the first man and woman. They sinned and had to leave the Garden of Eden and be separated from God.**

***Jesus* and the *cross* go together because Jesus died on the cross to take the punishment for all our sins. Through the faith God gives us, we are made holy and can be back with God again.**

The *tabernacle* and a *church* match because they are both sanctuaries, places where God dwells. The children of Israel worshiped in the tabernacle, and we often worship in a church.

***Baptism* and *water* belong together because through water and God's Word, our faith in God begins. Jesus dwells in our hearts through faith!**

***Bread* and *wine* are the way that Jesus is present with us during the Sacrament of Holy Communion. The word *communion* actually means "being together."**

***Music* and *praise* match because songs are one way we worship God in His sanctuary and thank Him for His goodness.**

***Hands* and *prayer* match because we often fold our hands to talk with God when we are in His house.**

***Glory* and *cloud* match. Long ago, the cloud over the tabernacle showed God's people His glory. When Jesus was on earth, He showed us God's glory. Now, as God's children, we are privileged to show God's glory as we serve others.**

Craft Page

To Prepare: You will need Craft Page 12 (Student Book) and scissors.

Cut apart the pieces of Craft Page 12. Use the craft in one of two ways. One side—the side with the large picture—can be worked like a puzzle. The other side, with words and pictures, can be used to play a matching game. The following pictures and words make a match: ***Adam*** with ***Eve, Jesus*** with ***cross, tabernacle*** with ***church, Baptism*** with ***water, bread*** with ***wine, music*** with ***praise, hands*** with ***pray,*** and ***glory*** with ***cloud***. To play, the children work with a partner and one set of cards. The children spread out all the cards facedown so that they cannot see the words. They take turns turning over two cards. If the cards go together and match colors, they keep that set and tell how the two things pictured go together. When one child cannot make a match, the other child takes a turn.

4 Closing (5 minutes)

To Prepare: Use the CD. Gather materials to send home. Use the sticker of God's house (Student Pack) along with Activity Page 12.

Gather the children for the Closing. Each week, follow the same routine.

Say **When you first came to Sunday School this morning, you did this activity.** Hold up Activity Page 12. **Now that you have heard how much God wants to dwell with you, add a sticker over the top of the house pictured.** Hold up a sample of the sticker. Distribute Activity Page 12 and the stickers. **When you come to church, you are coming to a special place where God meets you, forgives your sins, gives you the "food" of His Word, and hears your prayers. He wants to be with you!**

Sing "Abide with Us, Our Savior" (*SGL*, p. 60) or "O Sing to the Lord" (*LSB* 808; CD 2)

Say **Oh give thanks to the Lord, for He is good** (Psalm 107:1; CD 6).

2, 6

Challenge Encourage the children to invite a friend to God's house!

Pray **Dear God, thanks for loving me so much that You want to dwell with me. In Jesus' name, I pray. Amen.**

As the children leave,

Say **God loves to dwell with you!**

Reflect Children need time to adjust to new situations. It may take a month before they feel at home at your church if they have never before been regular attendees at worship. How can you help them to adjust to their new environment? Is there another family at church you could ask to befriend the new family and make sure they feel welcome and included?

Visiting a Friend's House

Whose house would you like to visit?
With whom do you like to spend time?
Draw a path through the maze so you and your friend can be together.

_______________________'s
house

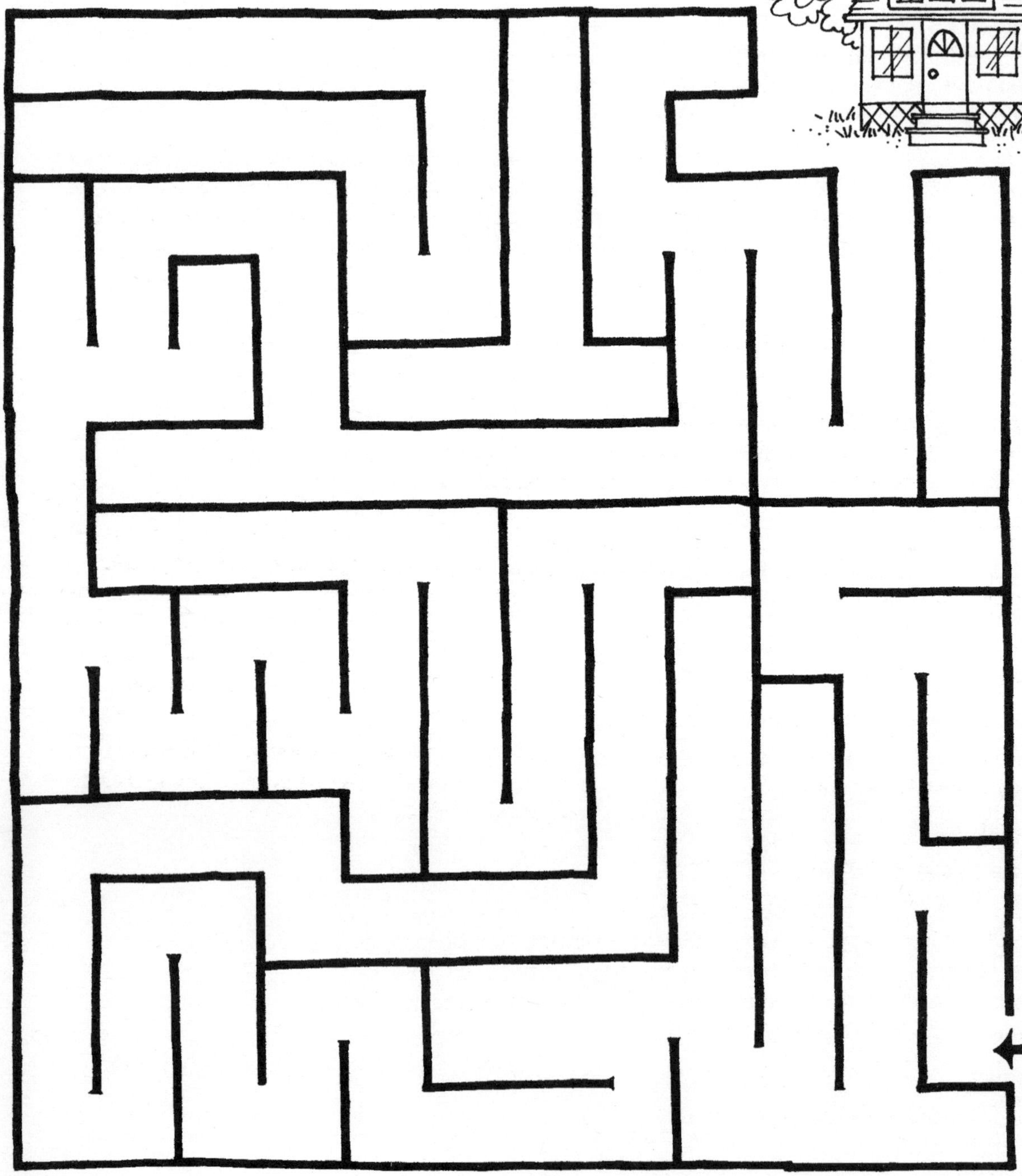

You

Extra: On the back of the paper, write a sentence or draw a picture to tell why you like to be there.

Lesson 13

Preparing the Lesson

Date of Use

The Bronze Serpent

Numbers 21:4–9

Key Point

As the bronze serpent was lifted up to heal and save the Israelites from the snakes, so Christ was lifted up on the cross to heal and save us from sin, death, and the devil.

Law/**Gospel**

Bitten and poisoned by sin and death, I complain when life is not what I want. **God calls me to repentance and points me to Christ, who heals me by His death and resurrection.**

Context

Forty years have passed since the nation began their wanderings as punishment for their rebellion (Numbers 13–14). A new generation is about to be given their chance to enter the Promised Land.

But like father, like son—their mouths are full of murmuring, for their hearts are overflowing with mistrust of God's benevolence. The woebegone desert in which they travel prompts them to throw a national pity party. After this incident, they will prove victor over enemy nations and encamp in the land east of the Jordan to prepare for Moses' farewell sermons (Deuteronomy) and their entry under Joshua's leadership.

Commentary

In Scripture, the snake is the devil's pet. Ever since Satan hissed his lies through that serpentine mouth in Eden, these reptiles have been demonized. Hardly does the Bible have a good word to say about them; in fact, quite the opposite. Even when Moses' and Aaron's staffs are transformed into snakes (Exodus 4:3; 7:9–12), they are hardly treated as "man's best friend."

It comes as no surprise, then, that of all the animals chosen to plague the grumbling, unbelieving Israelites in the desert, snakes were the chosen weapon. These were "fiery serpents," which probably refers not to their appearance (as if they were glowing) but to the effect of their venom on the human body. Not only did it burn, however; it also killed.

This is a radical call to repentance. But as the psalmist says, "When He killed them, they sought Him" (Psalm 78:34). Sometimes, one has to come face-to-face with death to face up to his or her sin and seek the face of the living God. So it was for Israel. So it is oftentimes for us.

The confession of the people is good and right. They have sinned against God and His chosen leader. But what they want is not what they need. They don't need a divine St. Patrick to clear their little desert Ireland of serpents.

Christ knows what they need: a visible conduit for His healing, a medicine that is in the very image of the problem itself. They need a serpent of salvation, and that's what God gives them. The bronze serpent, uplifted on the pole, is the means chosen to grant healing and relief. Under the guise of these deadly serpents, this bronze serpent works not death but life. Through it, Christ saves.

In John 3:14, Jesus says that as Moses raised this serpent in the wilderness, so He, too, must be lifted up on the cross to draw all men to Himself. Hidden under the guise of a condemned sinner is the Holy One of God. He has become our sin, *the* sinner, that we might become the righteousness of God in Him (2 Corinthians 5:21). Christ is our true "serpent of salvation," in whom we are healed from the venom of sin and death.

To hear an in-depth discussion of this Bible account, visit cph.org/podcast and listen to our Seeds of Faith podcast each week.

Lesson 13

The Bronze Serpent

Numbers 21:4–9

Connections

Bible Words
As Moses lifted up the serpent . . . , so must the Son of Man be lifted up, that whoever believes in Him may have eternal life. John 3:14–15

Faith Word
repentance

Hymn
O Sing to the Lord (*LSB* 808; CD 2)

Catechism
Apostles' Creed: First Article

Liturgy
Confession and Absolution
Sign of the cross

1 Opening (10 minutes)

Introducing Concepts

To Prepare: Post the attendance chart, and set out the offering basket and attendance stickers (Student Pack). Make a copy of Activity Page 13 (TG) at the end of this lesson for each child, and provide pencils (or crayons).

Greet your students as they arrive. Introduce yourself and other students to any new students. Direct the students to place their offerings in the basket and post their attendance on the chart with the stickers. Hand out Activity Page 13.

Ask **How do you get better when you are hurt or sick? Let's find out. Draw a line to connect the things that go together.**

As the students finish, they can gather together and talk about their answers. When you finish,

Say **In our Bible story for today, the Israelites get sick and need healing. Let's find out what happened and how God worked so that many were healed.**

MATERIALS NEEDED

1 Opening	2 God Speaks	3 We Live	4 Closing
Teacher Tools Attendance chart **Student Pack** Stickers **Other Supplies** Activity Page 13 (TG) Resource Page 1 (TG, optional)	**Teacher Tools** Poster E Glue stick **Student Pack** Lesson Leaflet 13 Stickers **Other Supplies** Lily puppet Candy bar or small toy Resource Page 2 (TG) Props for story (optional)	**Teacher Tools** CD **Student Pack** Craft Page 13	**Teacher Tools** CD

Rituals and Routines

To Prepare: If your children gather with others for the Opening, begin teaching with part 2. If you prefer to develop your own opening, a suggested outline follows. For an extended opening, use Resource Page 1 (TG).

Gathering Song: "Lord Jesus, Think on Me" (*LSB* 610; CD 1) or "There Is a Name I Love to Hear" (*SGL*, p. 50)

Invocation: **In the name of the Father and of the Son and of the Holy Spirit. Amen.**

Offering

The Commandments: Review the First Commandment (CD 19)

Prayers

Celebrations: Birthdays and Baptism birthdays

2 God Speaks (20 minutes)

Introducing God's Word

To Prepare: Set out a restickable glue stick (available from cph.org), the Faith Words Poster (Poster E), and the Faith Words cards (Resource Page 2) found in the back of the Teacher Guide. This week, cut out the word *repentance* from the cards. Have Lily the puppet on hand. Place a small candy bar or a small toy inside her satchel.

Teacher: Hi, Lily! *(Pause and look at Lily thoughtfully.)* What's wrong?

Lily: *(Sniffling)* Well, I feel bad about something. About the treat in my satchel.

Teacher: Lily, if you've got a treat, why are you sad?

Lily: I'm sad because I did something wrong. I cried and fussed because I wanted a treat. I whined and stomped my foot. Mom told me it was wrong to fuss, but I didn't care. Finally, when Mom wasn't looking, I asked Grandma, and she bought the treat for me. When Mom found out what I did, she was not happy. Once we got home, I had to go to my room for "think time." Now I feel bad. I was mean to Mom, and I'm sorry. *(Hanging head)*

Teacher: Did you tell your mom that you were sorry? I'm sure she'll forgive you. Maybe that would make both of you feel better.

Lily: *(Looking up)* You know, I bet you're right. I'll tell Mom I'm sorry. Bye!

Lily leaves. Show the Faith Words Poster (Poster E), and introduce today's Faith Word.

Say **This week's Faith Word is *repentance.*** Ask one of the children to use the glue stick to add the word *repentance* to the Faith Words Poster. **Lily was sorry for what she had done. When we are sorry for our sins, the Holy Spirit is at work in us. He leads us to confess what we have done wrong and, in faith, to turn to Jesus and ask for His forgiveness.**

In today's Bible story, the children of Israel grumble, God gets their attention, and they stop sinning. Let's find out what happened.

Telling God's Word

Say **Help me teach the Bible story. I will tell part of the Bible story, and you can join me when I sing a section, using the melody of "Jesus Loves Me."**

Today's Bible story is from the Book of Numbers. Show the location of today's story in your Bible. **The children of Israel had left Egypt and were wandering in the desert. While on their journey, they ate manna—a special food that God gave them from heaven. But they weren't happy. They complained to God about the water and the food.**

Now it's time to sing. Sing the following lyrics twice to the chorus melody of "Jesus Loves Me, This I Know" (*SGL*, p. 51).

Sing **We don't like manna! We don't like manna! We don't like manna! We hate this worthless food!**

Say **It was not good for the children of Israel to grumble and complain about the good things God had given them. God wanted them to stop. So He sent venomous snakes. Some people died from their snakebites. The snakes and their deadly bites made the people realize that they were sinning. The people told Moses that they were sorry for what they had done. Moses prayed to God for the Israelites.**

Sing the following lyrics twice to the chorus melody of "Jesus Loves Me, This I Know" (*SGL*, p. 51).

Sing **They are so sorry. They are so sorry. They are so sorry. Please take the snakes away!**

Say **Then, the Lord told Moses to make a fiery serpent, or snake, from bronze and place it high on a pole for all to see. After that, if a snake bit anyone, that person would look at the bronze snake and live.** Sing the following lyrics twice to the chorus melody of "Jesus Loves Me, This I Know" (*SGL*, p. 51).

Sing **God saved His people. God saved His people. God saved His people. He saves from sin and death.**

Lesson Leaflet Review

To Prepare: Hand out Lesson Leaflet 13, stickers for Lesson 13 (Student Pack), and a pencil to each child.

Discuss the illustration on the leaflet cover by answering the question provided. Then, open the leaflet to the interior pages. Use these pages to review the Bible story, or use simple props to act out the story. Work on the leaflet as a group. That way, everyone can be successful in sequencing the story's event.

Note: The snake on the pole gave life to the children of Israel who looked at it. Crosses, crucifixes, and the sign of the cross that the pastor makes over us at Baptism and in the Divine Service all remind us that Jesus has rescued us from sin, death, and the devil. Talk about the sign of the cross, and demonstrate how to make it.

Bible Words

As Moses lifted up the serpent . . . , so must the Son of Man be lifted up, that whoever believes in Him may have eternal life. John 3:14–15

To Prepare: Use the Lesson Leaflet to teach the Bible Words. As an option, draw a wide spiral pattern on a sheet of unlined paper.

Use the picture cues in the Lesson Leaflet to learn the Bible Words. Explain that the word *serpent* means "snake" and that Jesus used the words *Son of Man* to talk about Himself.

Option: Hand out the papers on which you have drawn the spirals. The children start in the middle (the snake's head) and write the Bible Words between the lines (the snake's body), turning the paper as they go. When they are finished, they can cut along the spiral to make a 3-D snake.

Ask **What do you notice about the picture cues at the bottom of the Lesson Leaflet?** (Both the snake and Jesus are lifted up.) **From what were the Israelites saved? From what does Jesus save us? Let's talk about it in our next activity.**

Key Point

As the bronze serpent was lifted up to heal and save the Israelites from the snakes, so Christ was lifted up on the cross to heal and save us from sin, death, and the devil.

3 We Live (20 minutes)

Growing through God's Word

To Prepare: Have on hand one piece of plain paper for each student and two extra pieces. On one of the extra pieces of paper, draw the head of a snake. On the other, draw the tail of a snake. Also provide crayons or markers.

Say **The children of Israel complained about the food and water that God gave them while they were wandering in the desert. We complain about things too. Let's think of some things that boys and girls complain about.**

Great Idea!

Distribute the paper and crayons or markers. Ask each child to draw a picture or write about something children their age might complain about. Offer suggestions such as kinds of food, styles of clothing, difficulty or amount of school assignments, problems with friends, or times they have to go to bed or get up. When the children finish, ask them to stand in a line. Ask the children to place their papers in front of them on the floor, side by side; add the tail of the snake to one end and the head of the snake to the other. When the snake has been formed,

Say **Look at our sin snake. We have all been bitten by the sin of grumbling and complaining. We don't recognize or appreciate that God gives us everything we need in life. At times, we want something else or something more.** If time permits, read the First Article and meaning; you may want to use the CD. You could even use a device to record several or all of the children explaining why those words are so important to remember and what they mean to them. Challenge them to explain what God gives us and why we can trust in Him and not complain. Use social media, the church website, or email to share the video with parents. As always, secure parental permission before posting something publicly, or limit access to those you invite.

Say **Let's wiggle our sinful snake.** Invite the children to wiggle the snake by moving their papers. **Sin separates us from God, but God loves each of you so much that He wants you to be close to Him.**

In love, God calls you to repentance—to be sorry for your sins. Take time to say each child's name. Say, **God's says, "[Child's name], I love you. I want to forgive you."** Tell the children to show that they repent by turning themselves in the opposite direction. **God gives you His power to repent and turn away from sin. As you do that, you turn in faith toward Him.** Ask the children to face you again.

During the church service, we confess our sins before God's altar. When we finish, the pastor turns from the altar to us. He speaks God's words of forgiveness. Through God's forgiveness, we receive life forever.

On the cross, Jesus died for all your sins, including the sins of grumbling and complaining. To remember that, let's use our snake pieces to make a cross.

The children move their papers to form a cross on the floor. When they are finished,

Say **We are forgiven sinners. We have the Holy Spirit's power to pray to God, to praise Him, and to give Him thanks.**

Review God's gifts through the words of the meaning of the First Article of the Apostles' Creed using Luther's Small Catechism.

Craft Page

To Prepare: Hand out Craft Page 13 (Student Book), scissors, and a glue stick to each student. While the children are working, play the CD.

Say **To help us remember that Jesus saves us from our complaining, let's make a cross and a snake using our Craft Page.** Read the following directions at an appropriate pace, watching to see how your students progress. **Cut along the solid black lines. Set aside the corner pieces. Fold up the craft on the dotted lines. The Bible Words will be on the bottom, serving as your base. Glue together the backs of the two folded-up pieces. Attach the snake on the pole piece to the side showing the children of Israel. Attach the Jesus on the cross piece to the opposite side.**

When the craft is completed, you will see a crowd of people looking up at the cross on one side and a crowd of people looking up at the snake on a pole on the other side.

4 Closing (5 minutes)

To Prepare: Use the CD. Gather materials to send home. Gather the children for the Closing. Each week, follow the same routine.

Say **God told Moses to have a bronze serpent made and lifted up to save the people of Israel from their punishment, which was death. We complain and sin too. We deserve to be punished too. But God rescued us. He sent Jesus. He was lifted up on the cross to save us from our punishment of death.**

Sing "God Loved the World So That He Gave" (*LSB* 571; CD 9) or "O Sing to the Lord" (*LSB* 808; CD 2)

Say **As Moses lifted up the serpent . . . , so must the Son of Man be lifted up, that whoever believes in Him may have eternal life** (John 3:14–15)**.**

Challenge Can the children keep from complaining all week long?

Pray **Dear God, I'm sorry for complaining. Forgive me for Jesus' sake. Amen.**

As the children leave, hold a picture of Jesus or a crucifix, and

Say **Look to Jesus. He saves you.**

Reflect Think about those students in your class who complain or cause the most distractions during class. How can you nurture them?

Healed

Look at the pictures. Draw lines to connect what hurts with what can help.

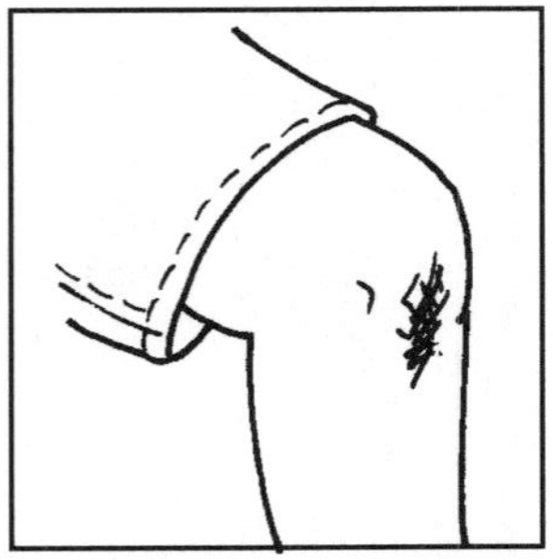

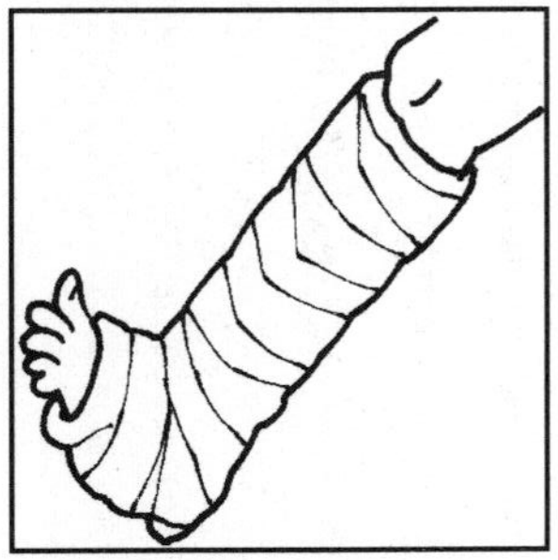

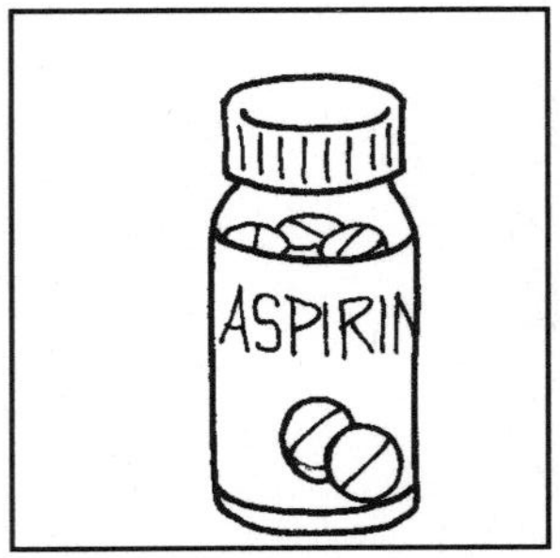

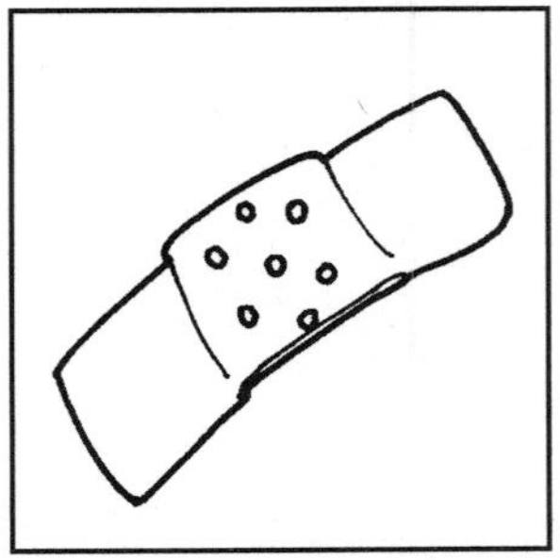

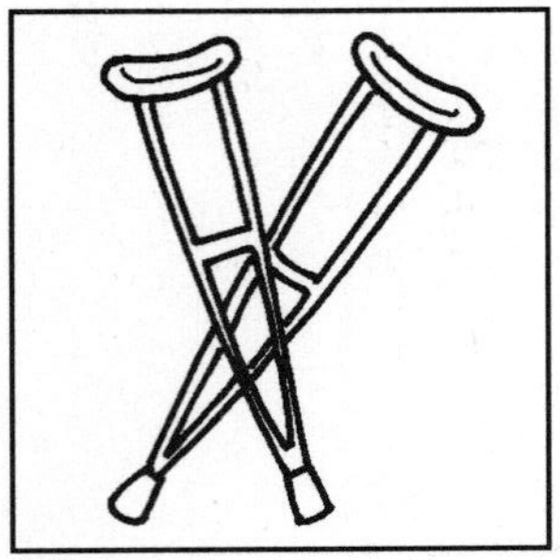

Bonus: We are sick because of sin. How are we saved from the sickness of sin, death, and the devil?

Opening

Sing a Gathering Song

Sing "Welcome, Welcome, All Who Come" (*SGL*, p. 89).

Say the Invocation

In the name of the Father and of the Son and of the Holy Spirit. Amen.

Show the children how to make the sign of the cross.

Tell about Colors and Symbols

What colors do you see? What symbols do you see?

Collect the Offering

Sing "Father, Bless the Gifts We Bring You" (*SGL*, p. 87).

Pray

Invite the children to bow their heads and fold their hands.

The Lord's Prayer

Luther's Morning Prayer (CD 23)

Other Prayers

Celebrate Special Days

Provide a small gift or sticker to those who are celebrating birthdays or Baptism birthdays.

For birthdays, sing "A Glad and Happy Birthday" (*SGL*, p. 90).

For Baptism birthdays, sing "I Was Baptized" (LOSP, p. 97).

